About the Author

Vijay Yadav is a passionate researcher, editor, and technology enthusiast with a deep interest in Artificial Intelligence, Automation, and Cybersecurity. With a background in medical research, **Vijay** has always been fascinated by the intersection of science and technology.

Beyond research, he has gained expertise **in video editing, coding, ethical hacking, and stock trading,** making him a multi-talented individual with a keen eye for emerging technologies. His journey into *AI & Automation* began with a curiosity to explore how machines can revolutionize industries, and this book is a reflection of his knowledge and insights.

Vijay believes that AI is not just a tool but a transformative force that can shape the future. Through this book, he aims to make complex AI concepts accessible to everyone, from beginners to professionals.

When he is not working on technology-driven projects, *Vijay* enjoys learning about new innovations, staying updated with the latest tech trends, and experimenting with automation tools.

Index

Chapter 1: Understanding AI

Artificial Intelligence (AI) is a branch of computer science focused on creating systems that can perform tasks typically requiring human intelligence. AI encompasses various technologies, such as machine learning, deep learning, and natural language processing, all of which allow machines to "learn" from data and make decisions without human intervention.

1.1 What is AI?

At its core, AI refers to machines designed to simulate human cognitive functions. These systems aim to solve problems, recognize patterns, learn from experience, and make predictions. AI can be categorized into two broad types:

Narrow AI: Specialized in one specific task (e.g., speech recognition, facial recognition).

General AI: An advanced form that can perform any intellectual task a human can do. This level is still theoretical.

1.2 How Does AI Work?

AI works by using algorithms and models to process large amounts of data. The machine learns patterns and makes predictions based on that data. This learning can be supervised (using labeled data), unsupervised (using unlabeled data), or reinforcement-based (learning through trial and error).

Examples of AI techniques:

Machine Learning (ML): A subset of AI where computers are trained using data to improve their performance over time. It is used in applications like email spam filtering and stock market analysis.

Deep Learning: A type of ML that uses neural networks with many layers to analyze data with a structure similar to how the human brain works. This is the technology behind self-driving cars.

Natural Language Processing (NLP): This allows machines to understand and interact with human language, enabling applications like chatbots, voice assistants, and translation services.

1.3 Applications of AI

AI is transforming several sectors by automating tasks, improving decision-making, and enhancing customer experiences. Some notable applications include:

Healthcare: AI is used in diagnostics, personalized medicine, and drug discovery.

Finance: AI models detect fraud, analyze market trends, and automate trading.

Retail: AI helps personalize shopping experiences, recommend products, and manage inventory.

Transportation: Autonomous vehicles rely on AI to navigate and make decisions on the road.

1.4 Challenges and Concerns

Despite its many benefits, AI faces several challenges:

Data Privacy: AI systems require vast amounts of data, raising concerns about how personal information is collected and used.

Job Displacement: Automation through AI could potentially replace jobs that were once carried out by humans, leading to job loss in certain industries.

Bias in AI: Since AI learns from data, any biases present in the data can be reflected in the decisions made by AI systems. This has led to concerns about fairness and discrimination, particularly in areas like hiring and law enforcement.

Chapter 2: Automation and AI

Automation refers to the use of technology to perform tasks without human intervention. It has been a key part of industries for decades, especially in manufacturing. However, the integration of AI into automation systems has taken it to a whole new level, allowing machines not just to follow predefined instructions but to also adapt and learn from their environment.

2.1 What is Automation?

At its simplest, automation replaces human labor with machines to complete tasks. Traditionally, this was achieved using mechanical and electrical systems. But today, AI is pushing automation further, making it smarter and more efficient. For instance, instead of just assembling products on a factory line, robots now use AI to optimize the process in real-time, adjusting based on the data they receive.

2.2 Types of Automation

There are several types of automation, each with its specific applications:

Fixed or Hard Automation: This is used for high-volume, repetitive tasks, such as mass production in factories.

Programmable Automation: This type allows machines to be reprogrammed to handle different tasks, often used in batch production.

Flexible or Soft Automation: This type involves machines that can adapt to changes in the production process, such as robots that can handle different products without needing a complete redesign.

2.3 AI in Automation

When combined with AI, automation systems can make decisions, analyze situations, and adapt to changing environments without human input. AI algorithms can process massive amounts of data in real-time, allowing automated systems to predict outcomes and optimize processes on their own.

Some of the major ways AI is enhancing automation include:

Self-Learning Robots: In manufacturing, AI-powered robots are not limited to predefined tasks. They can adjust their actions based on data and even learn new tasks by observing human workers or interacting with their environment.

Predictive Maintenance: AI in automation can predict when a machine is likely to break down and schedule maintenance accordingly, reducing downtime and improving efficiency.

Supply Chain Automation: AI can analyze data from suppliers, inventory levels, and customer demand, automatically making decisions about reordering, restocking, and logistics.

2.4 Examples of Automation in Action

1. Self-Driving Cars: Autonomous vehicles are a perfect example of automation and AI working together. These cars use AI to interpret the data from their sensors and navigate traffic without human intervention.

2. AI-Powered Chatbots: Chatbots use AI to handle customer inquiries, offering support 24/7. They can understand natural language, process requests, and provide relevant information without human agents.

3. Automated Warehouses: Companies like Amazon use AI-powered robots in their warehouses to move goods, pick orders, and even assist in packaging.

2.5 Benefits of AI in Automation

Increased Efficiency: Machines can work continuously without needing breaks, leading to increased productivity.

Cost Reduction: Automation reduces the need for manual labor, cutting costs in the long term.

Improved Quality: AI systems can ensure consistency and precision in manufacturing processes, resulting in higher-quality products.

Safety: Dangerous tasks can be automated, reducing the risk of injury to human workers.

2.6 Challenges and Concerns

While the integration of AI in automation offers numerous benefits, it also brings challenges:

Job Displacement: As machines take over more tasks, there's a concern about job loss in industries that rely heavily on manual labor.

Complexity in Implementation: Deploying AI in automation requires a significant investment in technology and infrastructure.

Ethical Concerns: The decision-making power of AI systems, especially in areas like law enforcement and military, raises questions about accountability and ethics.

Chapter 3: AI in Everyday Life

Artificial Intelligence is not just a distant concept—it is already embedded in our daily lives. From smartphones to smart homes, AI is increasingly making everyday tasks easier, more efficient, and personalized. In this chapter, we will explore how AI is transforming various aspects of our day-to-day activities.

3.1 AI-Powered Devices

Smartphones: AI is at the heart of smartphones, powering features like face recognition, voice assistants, camera enhancements, and predictive text. Apple's Siri, Google Assistant, and Samsung's Bixby are examples of AI-based personal assistants that help users manage tasks and access information effortlessly.

Voice Assistants: Virtual assistants like Amazon's Alexa, Google's Assistant, and Apple's Siri use AI and natural language processing to understand spoken commands, answer questions, and control smart home devices. They can set reminders, control music, and even shop online based on user preferences.

3.2 AI in Personalization

AI is helping brands personalize their products and services, making them more tailored to individual needs:

Recommendation Systems: Streaming platforms like Netflix and YouTube use AI to suggest content based on viewing history, preferences, and user behavior. This ensures that the recommendations are always relevant to the user.

E-commerce: Online shopping platforms such as Amazon and Flipkart use AI to recommend products to customers based on their past searches, purchases, and browsing patterns. These AI systems continuously improve the recommendations based on data collected from millions of users.

3.3 AI in Entertainment

AI has revolutionized the entertainment industry in several ways:

Movie and Music Recommendations: AI algorithms track user preferences on platforms like Netflix, Spotify, and YouTube, offering personalized recommendations for movies, TV shows, and music.

AI in Video Games: In gaming, AI controls the behavior of non-playable characters (NPCs) and adapts to a player's actions, offering a more immersive experience. AI also plays a role in creating procedurally generated environments and challenges in games.

AI-Generated Content: Platforms like OpenAI's GPT-3 are creating stories, scripts, and even music using deep learning. AI-generated content is expanding the horizons of creativity.

3.4 AI in Transportation

Transportation is one of the sectors seeing significant AI-driven changes:

Self-Driving Cars: Autonomous vehicles use AI to interpret sensor data and navigate streets. Companies like Tesla, Waymo, and Uber are at the forefront of developing self-driving cars that aim to make transportation safer and more efficient.

Traffic Management: AI is also being used to optimize traffic flow in cities. Through smart traffic lights and traffic prediction algorithms, AI systems can reduce congestion, improve traffic management, and shorten commute times.

3.5 AI in Healthcare

AI is making significant strides in healthcare, improving diagnostics, treatments, and patient care:

AI for Diagnostics: AI algorithms can analyze medical images (X-rays, MRIs) to detect diseases like cancer, heart conditions, and neurological disorders with remarkable accuracy. They can even predict the likelihood of diseases based on genetic and medical data.

Virtual Health Assistants: AI-powered health assistants like Babylon Health provide medical advice, book appointments, and even monitor chronic conditions. They allow patients to get instant consultations without the need to visit a doctor.

Drug Discovery: AI is accelerating the discovery of new drugs by analyzing vast datasets of chemical compounds and medical information, significantly shortening the drug development timeline.

3.6 AI in Education

AI is making education more personalized and efficient:

AI Tutors: AI-driven tutoring systems like Duolingo and Khan Academy's AI-based features help students learn at their own pace. These systems adapt to the learning style and pace of the student, offering personalized lessons and quizzes.

Grading and Assessment: AI is helping educators by automating administrative tasks like grading, which frees up time to focus on teaching. AI-based tools can grade multiple-choice questions, essays, and even provide feedback on student writing.

3.7 AI in Home Automation

Smart Homes: AI is used to power home automation systems that control lighting, security, heating, and cooling. Smart thermostats like Nest use AI to learn user preferences and adjust the temperature accordingly. AI-powered security systems, such as cameras that recognize faces and detect movement, can alert homeowners to potential threats in real-time.

Robot Vacuums: Devices like the Roomba use AI to navigate and clean your home. These robots learn the layout of your space and adapt to obstacles, ensuring efficient cleaning.

3.8 AI in Social Media

Social media platforms like Facebook, Instagram, and Twitter use AI to analyze user interactions and recommend content that is most likely to engage the user. AI also helps in detecting harmful content, such as hate speech and fake news, improving the overall user experience.

3.9 Challenges of AI in Everyday Life

While AI is making life easier, there are some challenges:

Privacy Issues: AI systems collect vast amounts of personal data, raising concerns about privacy and data security.

Dependence on Technology: Over-reliance on AI systems may lead to a lack of critical thinking and reduced problem-solving abilities in humans.

Bias in AI: Since AI systems learn from data, they can sometimes inherit biases from the data they are trained on, leading to unfair outcomes in areas like recruitment, healthcare, and law enforcement

Chapter 4: AI and the Future of Work

AI is not only transforming industries but also reshaping the workforce. While AI offers many opportunities for businesses to increase efficiency, reduce costs, and enhance productivity, it also brings challenges in terms of job displacement, skill requirements, and economic inequality. In this chapter, we will explore how AI is influencing the future of work and what it means for workers.

4.1 AI and Job Automation

One of the most discussed topics in AI is its potential to automate jobs traditionally performed by humans. AI-driven automation is expected to impact a wide range of industries, from manufacturing to services.

Manufacturing and Production: Robots powered by AI are already performing repetitive and dangerous tasks on assembly lines. They can assemble parts, package goods, and even conduct quality control. This reduces human error and increases efficiency.

Customer Service: Chatbots and virtual assistants are increasingly handling customer inquiries, reducing the need for human customer support agents. These AI systems can provide 24/7 assistance and handle multiple queries simultaneously.

Transportation and Logistics: Autonomous vehicles, drones, and AI-based logistics systems are transforming how goods are delivered. Self-driving trucks, for example, could replace long-haul drivers, while drones might replace couriers for small packages.

4.2 Impact on Employment

While AI may eliminate certain jobs, it also has the potential to create new roles. According to several studies, many jobs are being replaced, but AI is also expected to create jobs that didn't exist before.

Job Displacement: The automation of repetitive tasks in fields such as manufacturing, transportation, and administration will lead to job losses. For example, truck drivers, call center workers, and factory workers may see a reduction in job opportunities.

New Job Creation: As AI technology advances, new roles will emerge, such as AI specialists, data scientists, machine learning engineers, and robotics technicians. These positions will require workers to have a deep understanding of AI and automation technologies.

4.3 Skills for the Future

In a world where AI is becoming ubiquitous, there is a growing need for a workforce that is skilled in AI and automation. The types of skills needed will shift as traditional roles are replaced by AI systems.

Technical Skills: People with expertise in AI, machine learning, and data science will be in high demand. These skills will be necessary for developing, deploying, and maintaining AI systems.

Soft Skills: While technical skills will be essential, soft skills such as creativity, problem-solving, emotional intelligence, and communication will remain vital. These are areas where AI still falls short and will complement AI systems.

Lifelong Learning: Given the rapid pace of technological advancements, it will be crucial for workers to engage in lifelong learning. Continuous upskilling and reskilling programs will help workers adapt to new technologies and avoid displacement.

4.4 AI and Human Collaboration

AI is not meant to replace humans, but rather to work alongside them. Human-AI collaboration can lead to enhanced decision-making, increased productivity, and more efficient work processes.

Augmenting Human Capabilities: AI can assist humans by automating repetitive tasks, allowing workers to focus on more complex and creative aspects of their jobs. For example, in healthcare, AI can analyze medical images, leaving doctors more time to diagnose and treat patients.

AI as a Co-worker: In fields such as finance and marketing, AI tools are helping professionals make data-driven decisions. These AI systems can process vast amounts of data and offer insights that would be impossible for humans to generate manually.

Collaboration in Creative Industries: AI is also making waves in creative industries, assisting artists, writers, and musicians. Tools like AI-powered design software, content generators, and music composition programs help human creators achieve their visions more efficiently.

4.5 AI and Economic Inequality

The rise of AI and automation could widen the gap between the rich and the poor. Companies that adopt AI technology early will have a competitive advantage, while workers who are displaced by automation may struggle to find new opportunities without proper support.

Wealth Distribution: The benefits of AI may be disproportionately enjoyed by companies and individuals who own the technology. As automation reduces the need for human labor, wages for low-skill workers may stagnate, while high-skill workers with expertise in AI may see increased salaries.

Regional Disparities: AI could exacerbate existing economic disparities between regions. Developed countries that invest heavily in AI technologies may see faster economic growth, while developing nations may fall behind due to a lack of resources and infrastructure.

4.6 Preparing for the Future Workforce

To ensure that AI's impact on the workforce is positive, several steps need to be taken:

Education and Training: Governments and companies should invest in education and training programs to equip workers with the skills needed to succeed in an AI-driven economy. This includes both technical training and soft skills development.

Social Safety Nets: To mitigate the potential social impact of job displacement, stronger social safety nets, such as universal basic income (UBI) or retraining programs, could be implemented.

Collaboration between Stakeholders: Governments, businesses, and educational institutions need to work together to address the challenges of AI adoption and ensure that the benefits of AI are widely shared.

4.7 The Role of Government and Regulation

Governments will play a key role in shaping the future of work in an AI-driven world. Regulatory frameworks need to be put in place to ensure ethical AI deployment and protect workers' rights.

AI Governance: Governments will need to create policies that regulate AI technologies, ensuring that they are used responsibly and transparently. This includes creating standards for data privacy, ethical AI, and fairness.

Job Transition Policies: Governments must provide workers with the necessary support to transition into new roles, whether through retraining programs or social safety nets.

4.8 Conclusion

The future of work in an AI-driven world presents both opportunities and challenges. While AI has the potential to revolutionize industries, boost productivity, and improve quality of life, it also poses risks in terms of job displacement and economic inequality. By preparing the workforce for these changes through education, training, and social policies, society can ensure that AI's benefits are broadly shared and that workers are equipped to thrive in this new era.

Chapter 5: The Ethical Considerations of AI

Artificial Intelligence holds great promise, but it also raises important ethical questions. As AI systems become more integrated into various aspects of society, the potential for misuse, bias, and unintended consequences grows. In this chapter, we will explore the ethical considerations surrounding AI, including issues like bias, transparency, accountability, and the future of decision-making.

5.1 Bias in AI

AI systems are designed to learn from data, but the data they are trained on can often be flawed or biased. When this happens, the AI systems can inherit these biases, leading to unfair outcomes. This is a major ethical concern, especially in areas like hiring, law enforcement, and healthcare.

Data Bias: AI models rely on historical data to make predictions. If the data used to train the AI reflects existing societal biases (such as gender or racial biases), the AI may replicate or even exacerbate those biases in its decisions. For example, an AI used in recruitment might favor candidates from a particular demographic, reinforcing existing inequalities.

Algorithmic Bias: Even if data is neutral, the way an algorithm is designed can also introduce bias. If the developers unintentionally prioritize certain features or exclude relevant data, it can lead to skewed or unfair results.

Impact in Decision-Making: In fields like criminal justice, biased AI systems can lead to unfair sentencing or discrimination against certain groups. This has led to calls for more rigorous audits and testing of AI systems to ensure they are unbiased and fair.

5.2 Transparency in AI Systems

Transparency is essential to ensure that AI systems are understandable, trustworthy, and accountable. However, many AI models, particularly deep learning models, operate as "black boxes," meaning their decision-making process is not easily explainable.

The Black Box Problem: Deep learning algorithms are highly complex, making it difficult to understand how they arrive at specific decisions. This lack of transparency can create challenges in areas where accountability is crucial, such as healthcare or law enforcement.

Explainability: Researchers are working on making AI systems more interpretable and explainable. This is especially important in high-stakes situations, where individuals affected by AI decisions (such as patients or defendants) should be able to understand how those decisions were made.

Regulatory Requirements: Governments and regulatory bodies are pushing for transparency in AI systems, requiring companies to disclose how their algorithms work and the data they use. This helps ensure that AI systems are not making arbitrary or opaque decisions.

5.3 Accountability and Responsibility

As AI systems become more autonomous, questions about accountability become more complex. Who is responsible when an AI system makes a mistake or causes harm?

Liability: If an AI system malfunctions or causes harm (such as an autonomous vehicle causing an accident), it can be difficult to determine who should be held accountable. Should the developer, the manufacturer, or the user be responsible? Legal frameworks are struggling to address these questions.

Corporate Responsibility: Companies that develop and deploy AI systems must take responsibility for the ethical implications of their technologies. This includes ensuring that AI is designed and used in ways that benefit society, rather than causing harm.

Human Oversight: In many cases, it is essential for humans to remain in control of AI decision-making, especially in critical areas like healthcare or criminal justice. Human oversight can ensure that AI systems are used ethically and that their actions align with societal values.

5.4 AI and Privacy

As AI systems gather and analyze vast amounts of personal data, privacy concerns are becoming more pressing. AI can be used to track individuals, predict behavior, and even manipulate personal preferences.

Surveillance: AI-powered surveillance systems, such as facial recognition, raise concerns about privacy and civil liberties. These systems can track individuals without their consent, leading to potential abuses by governments or corporations.

Data Collection: AI requires large datasets to function effectively, but the collection and use of personal data can be invasive. Companies often collect data through apps, websites, and social media, raising concerns about how this data is used and whether it is adequately protected.

Data Protection Regulations: To address privacy concerns, governments have implemented regulations like the General Data Protection Regulation (GDPR) in the European Union. These laws aim to protect individuals' privacy and give them more control over their personal data.

5.5 AI in Autonomous Weapons and Military Applications

The use of AI in military applications raises significant ethical questions. Autonomous weapons, which can operate without human intervention, have the potential to change the nature of warfare and conflict.

Lethal Autonomous Weapons: These systems can make decisions about when and how to use force without human input. There are concerns about the potential for mistakes, lack of accountability, and the possibility of these weapons being used in unethical ways.

Ethical Warfare: The use of AI in warfare challenges traditional concepts of human responsibility and accountability. If an autonomous weapon kills innocent civilians, who is responsible—the AI system, the developers, or the military commanders who deployed it?

International Regulation: There is growing international concern about the development of autonomous weapons, with calls for treaties or regulations that restrict their use. The ethical implications of AI in warfare are an ongoing debate in international law.

5.6 AI and Human Rights

The deployment of AI has the potential to impact human rights, both positively and negatively. AI can be used to protect human rights by improving access to education, healthcare, and justice. However, it can also be used to violate rights, particularly when it comes to surveillance, discrimination, and the right to privacy.

Discrimination: AI systems, if not properly designed, can perpetuate discrimination, particularly in hiring, lending, and law enforcement. Discriminatory algorithms can prevent certain groups from accessing opportunities or receiving fair treatment.

Social Control: Governments or corporations could use AI to infringe upon individuals' rights to freedom of expression, privacy, and assembly. For instance, AI-based systems that monitor social media could be used to suppress dissent or political opposition.

Positive Use of AI: On the positive side, AI can also be used to track human rights abuses, provide access to education in remote areas, and improve healthcare outcomes, particularly in underserved regions.

5.7 The Future of Ethical AI

As AI continues to evolve, it is crucial that ethical considerations remain at the forefront of development. Developers, policymakers, and researchers must work together to ensure that AI is designed and used in ways that are fair, transparent, and accountable.

Ethical AI Design: AI systems should be designed with fairness and accountability in mind. This includes addressing issues like bias, ensuring transparency, and providing clear avenues for accountability when things go wrong.

Collaborative Efforts: Governments, academic institutions, and the private sector must collaborate to create ethical frameworks and standards for AI. This can include developing ethical guidelines, establishing oversight bodies, and ensuring that AI development aligns with human values.

Global Standards: Given the global nature of AI technology, international cooperation is needed to create consistent ethical standards that apply across borders. These standards can help ensure that AI benefits humanity as a whole, rather than being used to exacerbate inequalities or harm vulnerable groups.

Chapter 6: AI in Healthcare: Revolutionizing Medicine

Artificial Intelligence has the potential to transform healthcare by improving diagnoses, personalizing treatments, and enhancing overall patient care. From AI-driven diagnostic tools to robots assisting in surgeries, AI is making waves in various medical fields. In this chapter, we explore how AI is revolutionizing healthcare and what its future holds.

6.1 AI in Diagnostics

One of the most significant ways AI is impacting healthcare is in the field of diagnostics. AI systems can process and analyze vast amounts of medical data quickly, leading to faster and more accurate diagnoses.

Medical Imaging: AI-powered tools are used to analyze medical images, such as X-rays, CT scans, and MRIs. These tools can detect signs of diseases like cancer, tuberculosis, and heart conditions that might be missed by human doctors. AI algorithms can highlight areas of concern, allowing doctors to focus on these regions and make better-informed decisions.

Early Detection: AI can help detect diseases in their early stages, often before symptoms even appear. Early detection is crucial for effective treatment, particularly in diseases like cancer. For example, AI systems are being used to detect skin cancer from images of moles and lesions, providing early alerts for patients who may need further examination.

Genetic Analysis: AI is also playing a role in genetic research. AI tools are being used to analyze genetic data and identify mutations or patterns that might indicate a predisposition to certain diseases. This helps in personalized medicine, where treatments are tailored to an individual's genetic makeup.

6.2 AI in Personalized Medicine

Personalized medicine, or precision medicine, is an approach where medical treatment is tailored to the individual characteristics of each patient. AI is making personalized medicine more accessible by enabling the analysis of a patient's unique genetic and medical data.

Tailored Treatments: AI can help doctors design personalized treatment plans based on a patient's genetic profile, lifestyle, and environmental factors. For example, AI can recommend specific drugs or therapies that are more likely to be effective based on the patient's unique genetic makeup.

Predictive Analytics: AI algorithms can predict how a patient will respond to a particular treatment. By analyzing data from previous patients with similar characteristics, AI can suggest the most effective course of treatment. This can lead to better patient outcomes and fewer adverse reactions to drugs.

Treatment Monitoring: AI can also monitor a patient's progress during treatment, tracking various health metrics in real-time. This allows healthcare providers to adjust treatment plans as needed, ensuring the best possible outcomes for the patient.

6.3 AI in Drug Discovery and Development

The process of developing new drugs is long, costly, and complex. AI has the potential to speed up this process by analyzing vast amounts of data and identifying promising drug candidates more efficiently.

Drug Repurposing: AI can analyze existing drugs to determine if they could be used to treat other diseases. This process, known as drug repurposing, can significantly reduce the time and cost associated with developing new treatments. For example, AI has been used to identify potential treatments for diseases like COVID-19 by repurposing existing drugs.

Predicting Drug Efficacy: AI can help predict the effectiveness of new drugs by analyzing biological data, such as genetic information or molecular structures. AI models can simulate how a drug interacts with the body, allowing researchers to identify promising candidates before they are tested on humans.

Clinical Trials: AI can optimize the clinical trial process by identifying suitable candidates for trials, monitoring patient progress, and predicting trial outcomes. This can reduce the time and costs associated with bringing a new drug to market.

6.4 AI in Surgery: Robots and Automation

Robotic surgery is an area where AI has made significant advancements. AI-powered robots are assisting surgeons in performing complex procedures with greater precision and control.

Minimally Invasive Surgery: Robotic systems allow surgeons to perform minimally invasive surgeries, which involve smaller incisions and quicker recovery times for patients. These systems offer more precise movements, reducing the risk of human error during surgery.

Robot-Assisted Surgery: AI-driven robots, such as the da Vinci surgical system, allow surgeons to perform intricate surgeries with enhanced precision. These robots provide 3D visualization, fine motor control, and real-time feedback, all of which help improve patient outcomes.

Autonomous Surgery: In the future, AI may enable fully autonomous robotic surgery, where the robot performs the entire procedure without human intervention. While this may raise questions about the role of human surgeons, it holds great potential for increasing the speed and accuracy of surgeries.

6.5 AI in Patient Care and Monitoring

AI is also being used to enhance patient care outside of the operating room. From virtual assistants to wearable devices, AI can help monitor patients in real-time and assist in their daily care.

Wearable Health Devices: AI-powered wearable devices, such as smartwatches and fitness trackers, can monitor a patient's health metrics, such as heart rate, blood pressure, and activity levels. These devices can alert patients and healthcare providers to potential health issues, allowing for early intervention.

Virtual Health Assistants: AI-driven virtual assistants, like chatbots, are being used to answer patients' questions, schedule appointments, and provide health advice. These assistants can offer round-the-clock support, improving access to healthcare services and reducing the burden on medical professionals.

Remote Monitoring: AI can also be used to monitor patients remotely, particularly those with chronic conditions. For example, AI can track the vital signs of patients with heart disease or diabetes and alert healthcare providers if there are any concerning changes.

6.6 AI in Mental Health

Mental health is another area where AI is making strides. AI-powered tools are being used to diagnose, treat, and monitor mental health conditions.

Mental Health Diagnostics: AI tools can analyze speech patterns, facial expressions, and other behavioral data to diagnose mental health conditions like depression, anxiety, and PTSD. These tools can detect subtle signs of mental health issues that might be missed in traditional clinical settings.

Therapeutic Chatbots: AI-driven chatbots, such as Woebot, are being used to provide therapy and support to individuals dealing with mental health challenges. These bots can engage with patients in real-time, offering cognitive-behavioral therapy (CBT) techniques and providing emotional support.

Predicting Mental Health Crises: AI can analyze data from various sources, including social media and wearable devices, to predict mental health crises before they occur. By identifying warning signs, AI can help prevent suicide attempts or other serious mental health emergencies.

6.7 Ethical Challenges in Healthcare AI

While AI holds great promise in healthcare, its use raises several ethical challenges. These include issues related to privacy, accountability, and the potential for biased algorithms.

Privacy Concerns: Healthcare data is highly sensitive, and AI systems must be designed to protect patient privacy. Ensuring that AI systems comply with data protection laws and regulations, such as HIPAA or GDPR, is essential to maintaining patient trust.

Bias in Healthcare AI: AI systems can perpetuate biases present in the data they are trained on. If a dataset is not diverse enough, AI systems may not provide accurate or equitable care for all patients. Addressing bias in healthcare AI is a critical issue to ensure that all patients receive fair treatment.

Accountability and Trust: As AI systems become more involved in healthcare decision-making, it is essential to establish clear lines of accountability. If an AI system makes an incorrect diagnosis or treatment recommendation, who is responsible? Ensuring transparency and human oversight in AI healthcare applications is vital for maintaining trust.

6.8 The Future of AI in Healthcare

The future of AI in healthcare is exciting, with the potential to improve patient care, streamline operations, and reduce costs. As AI technology continues to evolve, we can expect to see even more groundbreaking innovations in medicine.

AI-Powered Diagnostics and Treatments: In the future, AI could become an integral part of the diagnostic process, helping doctors identify diseases with greater accuracy. AI may also be used to create more personalized treatments based on an individual's unique genetic profile.

AI and Global Health: AI has the potential to improve healthcare in developing countries, where access to medical professionals and resources is limited. AI-powered diagnostics, remote consultations, and personalized health advice could help bridge the healthcare gap and improve outcomes for millions of people.

Regulation and Ethics: As AI becomes more involved in healthcare, regulation and ethical standards will be essential to ensure that these technologies are used responsibly and for the benefit of patients.

Chapter 7: AI in Business and Industry: Transforming the Workplace

Artificial Intelligence is not only changing the healthcare and technology sectors but is also having a profound impact on businesses across various industries. From enhancing customer service to improving operational efficiency, AI is becoming an integral part of modern business strategies. This chapter delves into how AI is reshaping the world of business and the workforce.

7.1 AI in Customer Service

Customer service is one of the areas where AI has already made significant strides. AI-powered systems are improving customer experiences by providing instant responses, personalized support, and efficient problem resolution.

Chatbots and Virtual Assistants: AI-driven chatbots are being used by businesses to engage with customers 24/7. These bots can handle basic queries, direct customers to appropriate resources, and even process orders. Virtual assistants like Siri, Alexa, and Google Assistant have made their way into business, helping customers with various tasks, from booking appointments to troubleshooting issues.

Personalized Recommendations: AI algorithms are used to analyze customer preferences and behavior to provide tailored recommendations. Online retailers like Amazon and Netflix use AI to suggest products or movies based on previous interactions, enhancing the customer experience.

Predictive Customer Support: AI systems can predict customer issues before they arise by analyzing data from previous interactions. For instance, AI can monitor service usage patterns to identify when a customer might experience problems, enabling businesses to proactively address concerns.

7.2 AI in Marketing and Advertising

AI has revolutionized marketing by enabling businesses to create more targeted, personalized campaigns that resonate with their audiences. By analyzing vast amounts of consumer data, AI helps businesses understand consumer behavior and optimize their marketing strategies.

Targeted Advertising: AI is used to segment audiences based on demographics, interests, and online behavior. This allows businesses to run highly targeted ad campaigns, ensuring their message reaches the right people at the right time. Platforms like Facebook, Google, and Instagram leverage AI to optimize ad placements, maximizing the return on investment for businesses.

Content Creation: AI tools are now capable of creating content, such as blog posts, product descriptions, and even videos. For example, tools like GPT-3 can generate human-like text, allowing businesses to produce content more quickly and efficiently. AI can also analyze user engagement to suggest improvements and refine marketing strategies.

Customer Sentiment Analysis: AI systems can analyze customer feedback, reviews, and social media posts to gauge public sentiment about a product or service. This helps businesses understand how their customers feel, identify potential issues, and adjust their offerings accordingly.

7.3 AI in Supply Chain and Logistics

AI is transforming supply chain management by improving efficiency, reducing costs, and enhancing decision-making. With the ability to analyze vast amounts of data in real-time, AI is helping businesses optimize their operations.

Inventory Management: AI algorithms can predict demand and optimize inventory levels to ensure that businesses have the right amount of stock at the right time. This reduces the risk of overstocking or running out of products, ultimately improving the efficiency of supply chains.

Predictive Maintenance: AI-powered predictive maintenance tools are used to monitor the health of machinery and equipment. By analyzing data from sensors, AI can predict when equipment is likely to fail, allowing businesses to perform maintenance before a breakdown occurs. This helps reduce downtime and increase operational efficiency.

Route Optimization: AI can optimize delivery routes for logistics companies, reducing fuel costs and improving delivery times. By analyzing traffic patterns, weather conditions, and other factors, AI can determine the most efficient route for a delivery, helping businesses save time and money.

7.4 AI in Human Resources

AI is streamlining HR processes, from recruitment to employee engagement. By automating routine tasks and providing data-driven insights, AI is helping HR departments make better decisions and improve overall employee satisfaction.

Recruitment and Hiring: AI-powered tools are being used to screen resumes, identify top candidates, and even conduct initial interviews. These tools can analyze a candidate's qualifications, experience, and even their personality traits, helping businesses find the best fit for a role. This reduces the time and resources spent on manual recruitment processes.

Employee Retention: AI can analyze employee behavior and engagement levels to predict which employees are at risk of leaving the company. By identifying potential issues early, HR departments can take proactive measures to improve employee satisfaction and reduce turnover.

Performance Management: AI systems can provide real-time feedback on employee performance, helping managers make data-driven decisions. AI tools can track progress on goals, identify areas for improvement, and even recommend personalized development plans for employees.

7.5 AI in Financial Services

AI is playing a critical role in the financial services industry, helping businesses make smarter decisions, reduce risks, and enhance customer experiences.

Fraud Detection: AI algorithms are being used to detect fraudulent transactions by analyzing transaction patterns and identifying anomalies. Financial institutions use AI to monitor credit card activity, identify suspicious behavior, and prevent fraudulent activity before it happens.

Risk Management: AI is also used in risk management by analyzing financial data and predicting potential risks. For example, AI can help banks assess the creditworthiness of loan applicants, predict market fluctuations, and analyze investment portfolios.

Automated Financial Advisory: Robo-advisors are AI-powered platforms that provide automated financial advice based on an individual's goals and risk tolerance. These platforms use AI algorithms to analyze market trends and suggest investment strategies, making financial services more accessible to the general public.

7.6 AI in Manufacturing

Manufacturing is one of the industries that is benefiting most from AI. By automating processes, improving quality control, and optimizing production, AI is driving the next industrial revolution.

Smart Factories: AI is helping create "smart factories" where machines and systems are interconnected, allowing for greater efficiency and automation. These factories use AI to monitor production lines, predict maintenance needs, and optimize workflows in real time.

Quality Control: AI-powered systems can inspect products during the manufacturing process to ensure that they meet quality standards. These systems can detect defects or irregularities that might be missed by human inspectors, improving product quality and reducing waste.

Supply Chain Integration: AI is helping manufacturers integrate their supply chains, allowing for better coordination between suppliers, production teams, and distributors. AI can predict demand, optimize inventory, and ensure that products are delivered on time.

7.7 AI in Retail

Retailers are increasingly using AI to improve customer experiences, optimize inventory management, and enhance marketing strategies.

Customer Insights: AI tools are used to analyze customer data, providing retailers with valuable insights into shopping behavior and preferences. This allows businesses to personalize the shopping experience and create targeted promotions and offers.

Inventory Optimization: AI helps retailers optimize inventory by predicting demand and ensuring that the right products are available at the right time. This helps reduce overstocking and stockouts, ultimately improving profitability.

Virtual Shopping Assistants: AI-powered virtual assistants are being used in retail to provide customers with product recommendations, answer questions, and assist with purchasing decisions. These assistants improve the overall shopping experience, making it easier for customers to find the products they need.

7.8 The Future of AI in Business

The role of AI in business is expected to grow in the coming years. As AI technology continues to advance, its potential applications will expand, creating new opportunities for businesses across industries.

Automation and Efficiency: AI will continue to automate routine tasks, freeing up human workers to focus on more strategic and creative roles. This will lead to increased efficiency and cost savings for businesses.

Enhanced Decision-Making: AI will provide businesses with better data-driven insights, allowing for more informed and strategic decision-making. AI-powered analytics tools will help businesses identify market trends, optimize operations, and predict customer behavior.

AI and Innovation: As AI continues to evolve, businesses will be able to leverage its capabilities to create new products, services, and business models. AI-driven innovation will play a crucial role in helping companies stay competitive in an increasingly digital and interconnected world.

Chapter 8: AI and Automation in Everyday Life: Transforming Our Daily Routine

Artificial Intelligence and automation are becoming integral parts of our everyday lives, often in ways we don't even realize. From smart homes to autonomous vehicles, AI is reshaping how we interact with the world around us. This chapter explores the various applications of AI and automation in daily life and how they are making our routines smarter, more efficient, and more connected.

8.1 Smart Homes: The Rise of AI-Powered Living

AI has revolutionized how we manage our homes, offering smarter and more efficient ways to control various aspects of our living space. From lighting to security systems, AI-powered devices are making daily life more convenient.

Smart Assistants: Virtual assistants like Amazon's Alexa, Google Assistant, and Apple's Siri have become central to many smart homes. These devices use AI to perform tasks such as controlling the thermostat, playing music, setting reminders, and managing other connected devices, all through voice commands. They learn from user preferences and become more efficient over time.

Smart Appliances: AI-powered appliances, such as refrigerators, washing machines, and ovens, are designed to make household chores easier and more efficient. For instance, smart refrigerators can track food inventory and alert you when groceries are running low, while AI-enabled washing machines can automatically adjust settings based on the load and fabric type.

Home Security: AI is also improving home security. Smart cameras with facial recognition can identify familiar faces, while AI-driven alarm systems can detect unusual activity and send alerts in real-time. Smart locks and doorbell cameras allow homeowners to control access to their homes remotely, enhancing security and convenience.

8.2 AI in Transportation: The Future of Mobility

AI is revolutionizing transportation, offering safer, more efficient, and environmentally friendly ways to travel. From autonomous vehicles to intelligent traffic systems, AI is reshaping how we get from one place to another.

Self-Driving Cars: One of the most talked-about AI advancements in transportation is the development of autonomous vehicles. Self-driving cars use AI to navigate roads, avoid obstacles, and make decisions in real time. Companies like Tesla, Waymo, and Uber are actively developing self-driving technologies, which could lead to safer roads and more efficient transportation.

Smart Traffic Management: AI is being used to optimize traffic flow and reduce congestion. Smart traffic lights and AI-powered sensors analyze real-time traffic data to adjust signal timings, reducing wait times and improving traffic flow. In the future, AI could enable fully autonomous traffic management systems that make real-time decisions to improve road safety and reduce delays.

Public Transportation: AI is also enhancing public transportation systems. For example, AI can optimize bus and train schedules based on passenger demand, ensuring that public transit is more efficient and reliable. AI-powered apps provide real-time updates on schedules, routes, and delays, helping commuters plan their journeys more effectively.

8.3 AI in Healthcare: Personalized Care at Your Fingertips

AI is not just confined to hospitals and research labs; it's also becoming an integral part of personal healthcare management. AI-powered apps and wearable devices are making healthcare more accessible and personalized.

Wearable Health Devices: Smartwatches and fitness trackers, such as the Apple Watch and Fitbit, are AI-powered devices that help users track their health in real time. These devices monitor metrics like heart rate, blood pressure, and activity levels, providing valuable insights into an individual's health status.

Telemedicine and Virtual Health Assistants: AI-powered chatbots and virtual health assistants are changing the way people access medical advice. Apps like Babylon Health and Ada Health allow users to consult with AI-driven chatbots that assess symptoms and provide medical recommendations based on the information provided.

Personalized Medicine: AI is making personalized healthcare more accessible. By analyzing an individual's genetic information, lifestyle choices, and medical history, AI can help doctors develop tailored treatment plans that are more effective and efficient.

8.4 AI in Shopping and Retail: A Smarter Consumer Experience

AI is enhancing the shopping experience by offering personalized recommendations, improving inventory management, and making the overall shopping process more convenient for consumers.

Personalized Shopping: Online retailers like Amazon and eBay use AI to analyze customer behavior and offer personalized product recommendations. AI can suggest items based on past purchases, browsing history, and even social media activity, making shopping more relevant and enjoyable.

AI in Physical Stores: In physical retail stores, AI is being used to improve customer service and inventory management. Smart shelves equipped with sensors can track stock levels and automatically reorder products when they run low. In some stores, AI-powered robots are used to assist customers by guiding them to specific products or providing information about promotions.

Checkout Automation: AI is streamlining the checkout process. Self-checkout kiosks and automated cashier systems are becoming more common in retail stores. These systems use AI to scan items, process payments, and even handle returns, reducing wait times and improving customer satisfaction.

8.5 AI in Entertainment: Transforming How We Consume Content

AI is playing a major role in the entertainment industry, enhancing content creation, personalizing recommendations, and transforming how we consume media.

Content Recommendations: Streaming services like Netflix, Spotify, and YouTube use AI to recommend movies, shows, music, and videos based on user preferences. AI algorithms analyze your viewing or listening habits and suggest content that is likely to interest you, making it easier to discover new entertainment.

AI in Content Creation: AI is also being used in content creation, from video editing to music composition. For example, AI tools like Adobe Premiere Pro's Sensei use machine learning to automate tasks like color correction and sound editing, saving content creators time and effort. AI is also used to generate music and art, offering new creative possibilities.

Virtual and Augmented Reality: AI is enhancing virtual reality (VR) and augmented reality (AR) experiences, creating more immersive and interactive environments. AI can track user movements, adjust content in real time, and even generate realistic environments and characters, transforming how we interact with digital content.

8.6 AI in Communication: The Future of Interaction

AI is changing the way we communicate, making it easier and more efficient to interact with others, whether through messaging apps, emails, or voice assistants.

Voice Assistants and Speech Recognition: AI-powered voice assistants, such as Google Assistant and Amazon Alexa, are making communication more seamless. These devices can understand natural language commands and perform tasks like sending messages, making phone calls, and controlling smart devices.

AI in Messaging Apps: AI is enhancing messaging apps like WhatsApp, Facebook Messenger, and Slack by offering features like smart replies, chatbots, and translation tools. AI-driven chatbots can help users schedule appointments, order food, or answer frequently asked questions.

Translation Services: AI-powered translation tools, such as Google Translate, are breaking down language barriers by providing instant translations in real-time. These tools use machine learning to improve their accuracy, making it easier for people from different linguistic backgrounds to communicate.

8.7 AI in Education: Personalized Learning for All

AI is transforming education by providing personalized learning experiences, automating administrative tasks, and helping educators better understand their students' needs.

Personalized Learning Platforms: AI-powered platforms like Coursera and Duolingo are providing personalized learning experiences for students. These platforms adapt the content and difficulty level based on the learner's progress, ensuring that students can learn at their own pace.

AI in Classrooms: AI is also being used in classrooms to assist teachers and students. AI-powered tools can grade assignments, track student performance, and even provide real-time feedback to students. This allows teachers to focus on more strategic aspects of teaching and ensure that each student's learning needs are met.

Virtual Tutors: AI-driven virtual tutors are helping students with personalized tutoring sessions. These tutors can explain concepts, answer questions, and provide additional resources, making learning more accessible to students of all levels.

8.8 The Ethical Implications of AI in Daily Life

While AI is undoubtedly making life more convenient, it also raises important ethical concerns that need to be addressed. These include privacy issues, the potential for bias, and the impact on employment.

Privacy and Data Security: AI systems often rely on vast amounts of personal data to function effectively. This raises concerns about data privacy and the security of sensitive information. Ensuring that AI systems comply with data protection laws and respect user privacy is crucial to maintaining trust.

Bias in AI: AI systems are only as good as the data they are trained on. If the data is biased, the AI system may produce biased outcomes. This is a concern in areas like hiring, healthcare, and law enforcement, where AI systems may unintentionally perpetuate discrimination.

Chapter 9: AI in Business and Industry: Revolutionizing the Workforce

Artificial Intelligence (AI) is fundamentally transforming businesses and industries across the globe. From streamlining operations to creating more efficient workflows, AI is reshaping how businesses approach problems, innovate, and drive success. This chapter delves into the various ways in which AI is influencing business and industry, enhancing productivity, and creating new opportunities.

9.1 AI in Manufacturing: Automation and Precision

AI is revolutionizing the manufacturing sector by improving automation, precision, and quality control. Through the use of AI-driven systems, businesses are able to optimize production lines, reduce downtime, and increase overall efficiency.

Smart Manufacturing: AI-powered robotics and automation systems are being used to perform repetitive tasks in manufacturing. These machines can work faster and more precisely than humans, reducing the margin for error and ensuring consistent quality. For example, AI robots can assemble complex components in electronics, automotive, and even pharmaceuticals.

Predictive Maintenance: AI can predict when machines or equipment are likely to fail based on real-time data and historical patterns. This allows businesses to perform maintenance before problems occur, reducing downtime and preventing costly repairs. Predictive maintenance can be applied to everything from factory machinery to vehicles.

Supply Chain Optimization: AI is also enhancing supply chain management. By analyzing vast amounts of data, AI can forecast demand, optimize inventory levels, and identify the most efficient routes for distribution. This leads to cost savings and better resource allocation for businesses.

9.2 AI in Retail: Enhancing Customer Experience and Operations

The retail industry is increasingly adopting AI to improve customer experiences, streamline operations, and boost sales. From chatbots to automated inventory management, AI is enabling retailers to respond to customer needs more effectively.

Personalized Shopping: AI is improving the shopping experience by offering personalized product recommendations. By analyzing a customer's purchasing behavior, browsing history, and preferences, AI can suggest products that the customer is likely to be interested in. This leads to higher conversion rates and increased sales for retailers.

Chatbots and Virtual Assistants: Many retail businesses are using AI-powered chatbots to interact with customers. These virtual assistants can answer questions, process orders, and even assist with returns or refunds. AI chatbots offer 24/7 customer service, providing immediate assistance and enhancing customer satisfaction.

Inventory Management: AI systems are also improving inventory management by predicting demand patterns and optimizing stock levels. Smart algorithms can monitor inventory in real time and automatically reorder products when stocks are low, ensuring that businesses never run out of popular items.

9.3 AI in Finance: Revolutionizing Banking and Investment

The financial sector has been quick to adopt AI to enhance decision-making, improve security, and streamline services. From AI-driven algorithms in investment to chatbots assisting customers, AI is reshaping the world of finance.

Algorithmic Trading: AI algorithms are being used in the stock market to make investment decisions faster and more accurately than humans. These algorithms analyze vast amounts of market data in real time to identify trends and make investment decisions based on predictive models. Algorithmic trading has revolutionized the financial markets by enabling faster, more efficient trading.

Fraud Detection: AI is also being used to detect and prevent fraud in banking and financial services. AI-powered systems can analyze transaction patterns and flag any suspicious activity that might indicate fraud. This has helped banks and financial institutions reduce the risk of fraud and improve customer security.

Robo-Advisors: AI-powered robo-advisors provide personalized financial advice to clients, eliminating the need for traditional financial advisors. These systems use machine learning to analyze a client's financial situation, goals, and risk tolerance, then recommend an investment strategy tailored to their needs.

9.4 AI in Healthcare: Revolutionizing Patient Care

AI is transforming the healthcare industry by improving diagnostics, personalized treatment, and administrative efficiency. The use of AI technologies is enhancing patient outcomes and making healthcare more accessible.

Medical Imaging: AI is improving the accuracy of medical diagnoses by analyzing medical images such as X-rays, MRIs, and CT scans. AI-powered image recognition tools can identify patterns in images that may be missed by human doctors, enabling earlier diagnosis and more accurate treatment plans.

Virtual Health Assistants: AI is being used to provide virtual healthcare consultations. AI-driven health assistants can assess symptoms, provide medical advice, and even recommend treatments based on a patient's health history. This has made healthcare more accessible, especially in remote areas where doctors are in short supply.

Personalized Medicine: AI is helping to create personalized treatment plans based on an individual's genetic makeup, lifestyle, and health conditions. By analyzing patient data, AI can suggest the most effective treatment options, leading to better patient outcomes.

9.5 AI in Marketing: Enhancing Consumer Engagement

AI is transforming marketing by allowing companies to deliver more personalized and targeted advertising campaigns. By analyzing consumer data, AI is enabling businesses to tailor their marketing strategies and improve engagement.

Targeted Advertising: AI is being used to analyze consumer behavior and deliver personalized advertisements across various platforms. AI algorithms can predict what products or services a customer is most likely to be interested in and serve targeted ads that are more likely to result in a sale.

Customer Sentiment Analysis: AI is also being used to analyze customer feedback, social media posts, and reviews to understand consumer sentiment. This helps businesses gauge how customers feel about their products or services and make adjustments to improve their offerings.

Content Creation: AI tools are being used to generate content for marketing campaigns. From writing social media posts to creating blog articles, AI can help businesses produce high-quality content quickly and at scale. AI-driven tools like Copy.ai and Jasper are increasingly being used to generate copy that engages consumers and boosts conversions.

9.6 AI in Human Resources: Automating Recruitment and

Employee Management

AI is playing a key role in transforming human resources (HR) by automating recruitment processes, enhancing employee engagement, and improving workforce management.

Recruitment and Talent Acquisition: AI is being used to streamline recruitment by analyzing resumes, assessing candidate suitability, and even conducting initial interviews. AI-powered tools can quickly sift through thousands of resumes and identify the most qualified candidates based on predefined criteria, saving HR departments valuable time and resources.

Employee Engagement: AI-powered chatbots and virtual assistants are being used to enhance employee engagement. These tools can provide employees with instant access to HR policies, answer questions, and offer personalized recommendations for career development and benefits.

Predictive Analytics: AI is helping HR departments make data-driven decisions about employee performance, turnover, and engagement. By analyzing employee data, AI can predict which employees are at risk of leaving and suggest interventions to improve retention.

9.7 AI in Logistics: Improving Delivery and Supply Chain Efficiency

AI is playing an increasingly important role in logistics and supply chain management, optimizing routes, reducing delivery times, and improving overall operational efficiency.

Route Optimization: AI-powered algorithms are being used to optimize delivery routes for drivers. By analyzing traffic patterns, weather conditions, and delivery schedules, AI can suggest the most efficient routes, reducing fuel consumption and delivery times.

Warehouse Automation: AI-powered robots are being used to automate tasks in warehouses, such as sorting, picking, and packing goods. These robots can work faster and more accurately than humans, increasing the speed and efficiency of warehouse operations.

Demand Forecasting: AI is also being used to forecast demand in the logistics sector. By analyzing historical data, AI can predict when certain products will be in high demand, helping companies optimize their inventory and avoid stockouts.

9.8 The Future of AI in Business and Industry

The future of AI in business and industry is incredibly promising. As AI technologies continue to evolve, they will create new opportunities, drive innovation, and improve productivity across various sectors.

AI-Driven Innovation: In the future, AI will be at the heart of innovation in business. Companies will use AI to develop new products, services, and business models that were previously unimaginable. AI will help businesses stay competitive by enabling them to adapt quickly to market changes and consumer demands.

Collaboration between Humans and AI: Rather than replacing humans, AI will work alongside them to enhance capabilities. In the future, we can expect more human-AI collaboration in the workplace, where AI handles repetitive tasks while humans focus on creative and strategic work.

Ethical Considerations: As AI continues to reshape industries, businesses must consider the ethical implications of its use. Ensuring that AI is used responsibly, without causing harm or perpetuating bias, will be crucial to its widespread adoption.

Chapter 10: The Future of AI: Opportunities and Challenges

Artificial Intelligence (AI) has already begun transforming industries, economies, and societies. As AI technology continues to evolve, it presents both opportunities and challenges that need to be addressed to ensure a positive impact on the future. This chapter explores the future of AI, including its potential applications, the challenges it may bring, and how society can navigate this technological revolution.

10.1 The Potential of AI in Various Sectors

The future of AI holds vast potential for almost every sector of society. From healthcare to education, from entertainment to finance, AI is expected to drive innovation and efficiency across industries.

Healthcare Advancements: In the future, AI has the potential to revolutionize healthcare by enabling more accurate diagnostics, personalized treatments, and improved patient outcomes. AI-driven tools will be able to analyze medical data from various sources (e.g., genetic information, lifestyle, and medical history) to predict diseases before they manifest. Moreover, AI-powered robots could assist in surgeries, reducing human error and improving precision.

Education Transformation: AI will reshape education by enabling personalized learning experiences. AI-driven tutoring systems could adapt to the learning styles and paces of individual students, providing them with customized lessons. AI could also help educators by automating administrative tasks and offering insights into students' performance and areas of improvement.

Transportation and Mobility: The development of autonomous vehicles, powered by AI, will significantly change transportation. Self-driving cars, trucks, and drones could improve road safety, reduce traffic congestion, and lower transportation costs. AI-powered systems will optimize route planning, making transportation more efficient and sustainable.

Agriculture and Sustainability: AI has the potential to improve agricultural practices by optimizing crop production, reducing waste, and improving food security. AI-powered systems can analyze soil health, predict weather patterns, and recommend farming techniques to increase yield while minimizing environmental impact. Additionally, AI can contribute to sustainability efforts by improving energy efficiency, reducing waste, and developing cleaner technologies.

10.2 AI's Role in the Workforce of Tomorrow

As AI continues to evolve, it will play an increasingly significant role in the workforce. While some fear that AI will lead to mass unemployment, the future of work may be more collaborative than we think. AI will likely automate repetitive and mundane tasks, freeing up humans to focus on more creative and strategic roles.

Job Creation and Transformation: Although AI may displace some jobs, it will also create new opportunities. AI will open up new roles in fields such as AI research, data science, robotics, and machine learning engineering. Workers may need to upskill or reskill to adapt to the changing job landscape, focusing on skills that complement AI technology, such as problem-solving, critical thinking, and emotional intelligence.

Human-AI Collaboration: Rather than replacing humans, AI will collaborate with workers to enhance their abilities. AI can assist professionals by performing tasks that require speed, precision, and data processing. For example, AI can help doctors diagnose diseases faster, assist lawyers in contract analysis, and help engineers optimize designs. In this collaborative environment, humans will be able to focus on tasks that require creativity, judgment, and emotional understanding.

AI in Decision Making: AI will increasingly assist in decision-making across various industries, from business management to government policy. AI-powered systems can analyze vast amounts of data to provide insights and recommendations. For example, businesses can use AI to predict market trends, optimize supply chains, and make informed financial decisions. Governments can use AI to analyze social issues, optimize public services, and make evidence-based policies.

10.3 The Ethical Implications of AI

As AI continues to evolve, it raises important ethical questions that need to be addressed. While AI has the potential to bring tremendous benefits, it also presents risks that could have unintended consequences. Ethical considerations will be crucial in shaping the future of AI.

Bias and Fairness: One of the most significant ethical concerns surrounding AI is bias. AI systems are only as good as the data they are trained on, and if the data contains biases, the AI will perpetuate those biases. For example, AI algorithms used in hiring, law enforcement, or lending decisions could inadvertently discriminate against certain groups of people based on race, gender, or socioeconomic status. Addressing bias in AI systems will require diverse and representative data, as well as transparent algorithms.

Privacy and Surveillance: AI-powered technologies such as facial recognition and surveillance systems raise concerns about privacy. As AI is used to monitor individuals' behavior, movements, and activities, there is a risk that personal privacy could be violated. It will be important to strike a balance between the benefits of AI in security and safety and the protection of individual rights.

Autonomous Weapons: The development of autonomous weapons powered by AI raises serious ethical concerns. These AI-driven systems could be used in warfare, potentially making decisions to kill without human intervention. The use of autonomous weapons could lead to new forms of conflict, where the line between human accountability and machine decision-making becomes blurred. International regulations will be needed to address the ethical implications of AI in warfare.

AI Governance: As AI becomes more widespread, governments and organizations will need to establish clear regulations and guidelines to ensure that AI is developed and used responsibly. AI governance should prioritize transparency, accountability, and ethical considerations in the development and deployment of AI technologies.

10.4 Challenges in AI Adoption

Despite its potential, AI adoption comes with challenges that must be overcome to unlock its full benefits. These challenges include technical, societal, and economic barriers.

Technical Challenges: While AI has made significant progress in recent years, there are still many technical challenges to overcome. AI systems require large amounts of data to learn and make accurate predictions, and the quality of data is critical to the success of AI applications. Additionally, AI models can be computationally expensive, requiring advanced hardware and infrastructure that may not be accessible to all businesses and countries.

Societal Resistance: AI adoption may face resistance from certain segments of society, particularly in industries where jobs are at risk of automation. Workers may fear losing their livelihoods to machines, leading to social unrest and resistance to AI integration. Addressing these concerns will require policies that support reskilling, job creation, and economic transition for workers affected by AI.

Economic Inequality: The benefits of AI may not be equally distributed, leading to potential economic inequality. Large corporations and developed countries may be better positioned to harness the power of AI, while smaller businesses and developing nations may face challenges in adopting AI technologies. Ensuring that AI benefits all sectors of society will require international cooperation and investments in AI education and infrastructure.

10.5 AI and the Future of Humanity

The future of AI will not just impact industries and economies, but also the very fabric of human existence. As AI continues to advance, it raises profound questions about the role of humans in a world increasingly dominated by intelligent machines.

AI and Human Enhancement: AI could lead to advancements in human enhancement, such as brain-computer interfaces, augmented reality, and cognitive enhancements. These technologies could improve human capabilities, allowing people to access vast amounts of information, enhance memory, or even communicate directly with machines. While this may improve quality of life, it also raises questions about inequality, privacy, and the potential for misuse.

The Singularity: The concept of the "singularity" refers to a point in the future when AI surpasses human intelligence, leading to unpredictable and potentially radical changes in society. While the singularity is still a speculative idea, it raises important philosophical questions about the nature of intelligence, consciousness, and the relationship between humans and machines.

Humanity's Role in a Digital Future: As AI continues to evolve, it will be essential for humanity to define its role in a world where machines are capable of performing tasks that were once thought to be uniquely human. Will humans retain their place as the most intelligent beings on Earth, or will AI eventually take over decision-making in all aspects of life? The answers to these questions will shape the future of humanity in a world dominated by AI.

10.6 Conclusion

The future of AI holds immense promise, offering opportunities to enhance human lives, drive economic growth, and solve some of the world's most pressing challenges. However, it also presents risks and challenges that must be carefully navigated. The key to realizing the full potential of AI lies in responsible development, ethical considerations, and a commitment to inclusivity and fairness.

As AI continues to evolve, it will be essential for governments, businesses, and individuals to collaborate in shaping a future where AI is used to benefit society as a whole. The path forward will require a balance between innovation, regulation, and human values to ensure that AI serves as a force for good in the world.

Chapter 11: AI Ethics and Governance: Navigating the Future

As Artificial Intelligence (AI) continues to evolve and become more integrated into various aspects of life, ensuring its ethical use and proper governance becomes increasingly critical. AI's potential to impact every sector—from healthcare to finance, education to security—brings not only benefits but also significant challenges. This chapter explores the ethical concerns surrounding AI, the need for proper governance, and the frameworks that can guide its development and deployment in ways that ensure fairness, accountability, and transparency.

11.1 The Ethical Dilemmas of AI

AI presents several ethical dilemmas that need to be addressed to ensure its responsible use. These concerns arise from how AI is developed, used, and controlled, and they touch on issues such as privacy, accountability, and the potential for bias in decision-making.

Bias and Discrimination: One of the most prominent ethical concerns with AI is its potential to perpetuate and even amplify biases present in the data it learns from. If an AI system is trained on biased data, it can replicate these biases in its predictions or decisions. For example, AI used in hiring processes or loan approvals might inadvertently favor certain demographics over others based on historical biases in the data. Addressing bias requires diverse and representative datasets, as well as continuous monitoring and auditing of AI systems.

Transparency and Accountability: AI systems, especially deep learning models, are often referred to as "black boxes" because they make decisions in ways that are not easily understandable by humans. This lack of transparency can make it difficult to hold AI systems accountable for their actions, especially when they cause harm. For instance, in autonomous driving systems, if an AI-driven vehicle causes an accident, it may not be clear whether the fault lies with the algorithm, the developer, or the data used. Establishing clear accountability structures for AI systems is crucial to ensure that responsible parties can be identified in case of errors or harm.

Privacy and Data Protection: AI systems require large amounts of data to function effectively, often including personal and sensitive information. This raises concerns about privacy, data ownership, and how data is collected, stored, and used. AI applications in surveillance, for instance, may infringe on personal privacy, leading to potential misuse. It's essential to implement strong data protection laws and ensure that AI systems respect users' privacy rights while balancing the need for data-driven innovation.

Autonomous Weapons and Warfare: The development of autonomous weapons powered by AI has sparked widespread ethical debates. These systems could make life-and-death decisions in military contexts, potentially without human intervention. This raises serious concerns about accountability, as well as the possibility of AI-driven warfare, which could make conflicts more unpredictable and deadly. The question remains: Should machines be entrusted with the power to make decisions about life and death in war?

11.2 AI Governance: The Need for Regulation

As AI technologies grow more advanced and pervasive, the need for effective governance and regulation becomes paramount. Without proper oversight, AI could lead to negative social, economic, and political consequences. Therefore, governments, international organizations, and the private sector must collaborate to establish comprehensive AI regulations that address ethical concerns and ensure the responsible development and deployment of AI technologies.

Establishing Global Standards: To ensure that AI development is aligned with ethical principles, global standards and guidelines must be created. International organizations such as the United Nations and the European Union are already working on establishing frameworks for AI governance. These frameworks aim to set universal principles for AI design, transparency, accountability, and fairness. Global cooperation is essential because AI technologies transcend national borders and impact everyone, regardless of geographic location.

AI Regulation and Policy: Governments must create regulations that ensure AI technologies are used responsibly, safely, and ethically. These regulations should govern how AI is developed, tested, and deployed in various sectors, including healthcare, finance, and transportation. Regulations should include provisions for data protection, privacy, and the prevention of harmful outcomes, such as job displacement or the misuse of AI in surveillance.

AI Audits and Certifications: To ensure accountability and transparency, AI systems should undergo regular audits and certifications. These audits would assess the performance, fairness, and safety of AI systems and provide insights into their decision-making processes. Independent third parties can conduct these audits to ensure that AI systems comply with established ethical and regulatory standards. This would help mitigate risks associated with AI errors, biases, and malicious use.

Ethical AI Design: Developers play a crucial role in the ethical design of AI systems. By integrating ethical considerations into the AI development process—such as fairness, transparency, and accountability—developers can help mitigate the potential harms of AI. The use of explainable AI (XAI) is one such approach, allowing AI systems to make decisions in ways that humans can understand and interpret. Ensuring that AI systems are designed with ethical principles in mind will foster trust and acceptance among users and stakeholders.

11.3 The Role of Governments in AI Ethics and Governance

Governments play a critical role in shaping the ethical and regulatory landscape for AI. They are responsible for enacting laws that protect citizens' rights and ensure that AI is developed in ways that benefit society as a whole. Additionally, governments are instrumental in fostering innovation by providing the necessary infrastructure and support for AI research and development.

Creating Ethical Guidelines for AI: Governments should establish ethical guidelines for the use of AI that prioritize human welfare, equity, and social justice. These guidelines should address key issues such as data privacy, discrimination, and AI transparency. By creating these ethical frameworks, governments can help steer the development of AI technologies in directions that are beneficial to society.

Investing in AI Research and Education: Governments should invest in AI research and education to ensure that AI technologies are developed with a deep understanding of their potential impacts on society. By supporting research in AI ethics, fairness, and explainability, governments can help foster a responsible AI ecosystem. Education and training programs for AI developers and policymakers are also essential to equip them with the knowledge and skills to navigate the ethical challenges posed by AI.

Collaborating with International Bodies: Given the global nature of AI technologies, international collaboration is essential to establish coherent regulations and ethical standards. Governments should work together with international organizations, research institutions, and tech companies to create global frameworks for AI governance. This cooperation can help ensure that AI is developed in ways that promote global peace, security, and prosperity.

11.4 Corporate Responsibility and AI Ethics

While governments have a central role in AI governance, private corporations that develop and deploy AI technologies also bear significant responsibility. Tech companies must take proactive steps to ensure that their AI systems are ethical, fair, and transparent. Corporate responsibility in AI development goes beyond simply complying with regulations—it involves creating products that prioritize the well-being of users and society.

AI Ethics Committees: Many technology companies are establishing AI ethics committees to oversee the development of AI systems and ensure that ethical considerations are integrated throughout the product lifecycle. These committees consist of experts from diverse fields, including AI research, ethics, law, and social science, who work together to address the ethical challenges posed by AI.

Ethical Decision-Making Frameworks: Companies should adopt ethical decision-making frameworks that help guide their AI development processes. These frameworks can ensure that AI systems are designed and deployed with fairness, transparency, and accountability in mind. Additionally, companies should prioritize diversity in their AI teams to reduce the risk of bias and ensure that AI systems are developed to serve a wide range of users.

AI Transparency and Accountability: Corporations should prioritize transparency in their AI systems. This includes providing clear explanations of how AI models make decisions, disclosing the data used to train them, and making their AI systems auditable. Transparency builds trust with users and helps ensure that AI systems are used responsibly.

11.5 AI for Social Good: Ensuring Positive Impact

While there are risks associated with AI, the technology also offers tremendous potential to address some of society's most pressing challenges. By aligning AI development with the goal of social good, we can harness its power to tackle global issues such as climate change, poverty, healthcare, and education.

AI for Climate Change: AI can play a crucial role in mitigating the effects of climate change. From optimizing energy usage in buildings to predicting extreme weather events, AI can help reduce greenhouse gas emissions, improve resource management, and promote sustainable practices. AI-powered systems can also contribute to environmental monitoring and conservation efforts.

AI for Healthcare and Poverty Alleviation: AI has the potential to improve healthcare outcomes, particularly in developing countries. AI-driven diagnostic tools can help detect diseases early, even in remote areas with limited access to healthcare professionals. Additionally, AI can support efforts to combat poverty by optimizing resource allocation and improving access to education and financial services.

AI for Disaster Relief and Crisis Management: AI can enhance disaster relief efforts by providing real-time data analysis, improving coordination, and optimizing resource distribution during crises. AI can help governments and humanitarian organizations respond more effectively to natural disasters, conflicts, and humanitarian emergencies.

11.6 Conclusion: A Balanced Approach to AI Ethics and Governance

The future of AI holds immense promise, but it also presents significant ethical and governance challenges. Addressing these challenges requires a collaborative effort from governments, businesses, developers, and society as a whole. By establishing clear ethical guidelines, implementing robust governance frameworks, and ensuring transparency and accountability, we can guide AI development in ways that benefit humanity.

AI has the potential to drive innovation, improve quality of life, and tackle global challenges, but only if it is developed and used responsibly. By taking a balanced approach to AI ethics and governance, we can ensure that AI serves as a force for good, advancing both technological progress and human well-being.

Chapter 12: The Future of AI and Automation: Emerging Trends and Innovations

The future of Artificial Intelligence (AI) and automation is full of exciting possibilities. As technologies continue to evolve rapidly, the impact of AI on industries, society, and the economy is expected to become more profound. In this chapter, we explore the emerging trends and innovations in AI and automation, examining how they will shape the world in the coming years. From advancements in machine learning to the integration of AI with other technologies, the future promises significant breakthroughs.

12.1 Advancements in Machine Learning

Machine Learning (ML), a subset of AI, has seen incredible progress over the past few years. With new algorithms and improved computing power, ML systems are becoming more efficient and capable of solving increasingly complex problems. In the future, machine learning will continue to advance in several key areas:

Deep Learning: Deep learning models, inspired by the structure of the human brain, are expected to become even more powerful. These models are capable of learning from vast amounts of data, enabling them to perform tasks such as image recognition, natural language processing, and predictive analytics with incredible accuracy. Deep learning will be central to the next generation of AI applications, including autonomous vehicles, personalized healthcare, and advanced robotics.

Reinforcement Learning: Reinforcement learning (RL) is a type of machine learning where an agent learns by interacting with its environment and receiving feedback. RL has shown promise in areas such as robotics and game playing, and its applications are expanding. In the future, RL could revolutionize industries by enabling machines to adapt to dynamic environments and optimize decision-making in real-time.

Quantum Machine Learning: Quantum computing holds the potential to revolutionize machine learning. By leveraging the principles of quantum mechanics, quantum computers can process information in ways that classical computers cannot. Quantum machine learning (QML) aims to combine quantum computing and ML to solve problems that are currently intractable. As quantum computing becomes more viable, QML could open up new frontiers in AI research and innovation.

12.2 AI in Healthcare: Personalized Medicine and Diagnostics

AI is poised to revolutionize the healthcare industry, particularly in the areas of personalized medicine and diagnostics. Machine learning algorithms can analyze patient data, genetic information, and medical records to provide tailored treatments and predict potential health issues before they arise.

Personalized Medicine: AI can analyze vast amounts of medical data to help doctors provide personalized treatment plans for patients. By taking into account a patient's genetics, lifestyle, and medical history, AI can help identify the most effective treatments, minimizing side effects and improving outcomes. As AI continues to improve, personalized medicine will become more accessible and affordable.

AI-Driven Diagnostics: AI-powered diagnostic tools are already being used to detect diseases such as cancer, heart conditions, and neurological disorders. These tools analyze medical images, such as X-rays and MRIs, to identify abnormalities and provide early warnings of potential health issues. In the future, AI-driven diagnostics could become a standard part of medical practice, enabling doctors to make more accurate and timely diagnoses.

AI in Drug Discovery: The process of developing new drugs is time-consuming and expensive. AI can accelerate this process by analyzing chemical compounds and predicting their effectiveness. By using machine learning algorithms to simulate how drugs will interact with the body, AI can help identify promising candidates for further testing, reducing the time and cost of bringing new drugs to market.

12.3 AI and Robotics: The Rise of Autonomous Machines

The integration of AI with robotics is transforming industries and creating new opportunities for automation. In the future, robots powered by AI will be able to perform complex tasks with greater precision, efficiency, and autonomy. Key areas of impact include:

Autonomous Vehicles: Self-driving cars, trucks, and drones are set to become a common sight on roads and in the air. AI is already powering autonomous vehicles, enabling them to navigate and make decisions in real-time based on sensor data. As technology improves, autonomous vehicles will become safer and more reliable, reducing traffic accidents, improving transportation efficiency, and lowering emissions.

Industrial Automation: AI-powered robots are already being used in manufacturing to perform repetitive tasks such as assembly, packaging, and quality control. In the future, robots will become more adaptable and capable of handling a wider range of tasks. This will lead to increased efficiency in industries such as automotive, electronics, and logistics, as well as the creation of new job opportunities in robot design, maintenance, and programming.

Healthcare Robotics: Robotics combined with AI is also transforming healthcare. Surgical robots, powered by AI, can perform precise operations with minimal human intervention. AI-powered robots are also being used in elderly care, assisting with daily tasks and providing companionship to improve the quality of life for seniors. As robotics technology advances, healthcare robotics will continue to evolve, providing even greater assistance and improving patient outcomes.

12.4 AI and the Future of Work: Automation and Human Collaboration

The rise of AI and automation raises important questions about the future of work. While automation will undoubtedly lead to job displacement in some sectors, it will also create new opportunities and redefine how humans work alongside machines.

Job Transformation: Many jobs, especially those involving repetitive tasks, will be automated, but this will also open up new roles that require human creativity, empathy, and complex problem-solving. For example, while robots may handle routine manufacturing tasks, humans will be needed for roles that involve innovation, decision-making, and managing AI systems. Workers will need to adapt to new technologies and acquire new skills to remain competitive in the workforce.

Human-AI Collaboration: Rather than replacing humans, AI is likely to augment human capabilities. In industries such as healthcare, finance, and education, AI can assist workers by providing insights, analyzing data, and automating routine tasks. This will allow humans to focus on higher-level decision-making and tasks that require emotional intelligence and creativity. The future of work will involve collaboration between humans and AI, leading to more productive and efficient workplaces.

AI and Education: The integration of AI in education will personalize learning experiences for students. AI-powered tutoring systems can provide individualized feedback, identify areas where students need improvement, and recommend tailored learning materials. This will enable a more adaptive and inclusive educational system, where students can learn at their own pace and according to their unique needs.

12.5 The Ethical and Social Implications of AI and Automation

As AI and automation continue to advance, it is essential to consider their ethical and social implications. These technologies have the potential to disrupt economies, alter societal structures, and raise important questions about fairness, privacy, and accountability.

Job Displacement and Inequality: One of the biggest concerns about AI and automation is the potential for widespread job displacement. While automation will create new jobs, it may also exacerbate inequality by disproportionately affecting low-skill workers and certain industries. Governments and businesses will need to invest in retraining programs and create policies that support workers who are displaced by automation.

AI Bias and Discrimination: As AI systems become more integrated into society, there is a risk that they could perpetuate existing biases and inequalities. For example, AI systems trained on biased data may make unfair decisions in areas such as hiring, lending, and criminal justice. It is crucial to develop AI systems that are fair, transparent, and accountable, and to ensure that they do not exacerbate social inequalities.

Privacy and Surveillance: As AI technologies become more prevalent, concerns about privacy and surveillance are growing. AI-powered systems are capable of collecting and analyzing vast amounts of personal data, raising questions about how this data is used and who has access to it. Governments and companies must implement strict privacy policies to protect individuals' rights and ensure that AI technologies are used ethically.

12.6 Conclusion: Embracing the Future of AI and Automation

The future of AI and automation holds immense potential to transform industries, improve lives, and solve global challenges. However, it is crucial that these technologies are developed and deployed responsibly, with careful consideration of their ethical, social, and economic implications.

By embracing the opportunities presented by AI and automation while addressing their challenges, we can create a future where technology enhances human capabilities and drives positive change. The key will be to foster innovation while ensuring that AI benefits everyone and is aligned with the values of fairness, equity, and accountability.

Chapter 13: AI and Automation in Everyday Life: Impact on Personal Experiences

Artificial Intelligence (AI) and automation have increasingly integrated into our daily lives, often in ways that are not immediately obvious but have a profound impact on our personal experiences. From personal assistants on our smartphones to automated recommendations on streaming platforms, AI is changing how we live, work, and interact with technology. In this chapter, we explore how AI and automation are enhancing everyday life and transforming the way we interact with the world around us.

13.1 Smart Home Technologies

One of the most visible applications of AI and automation in everyday life is the rise of smart home technologies. These technologies use AI to create more efficient, comfortable, and secure living environments.

Voice Assistants: Devices like Amazon Alexa, Google Assistant, and Apple's Siri have become an integral part of many households. These voice-activated assistants use AI to understand commands and perform tasks like controlling smart devices, setting reminders, playing music, and answering questions. As AI improves, these voice assistants are becoming more intuitive, capable of understanding natural language and even detecting emotions.

Smart Thermostats and Lighting: Smart thermostats, such as the Nest Thermostat, use AI to learn your heating and cooling preferences over time. They can automatically adjust temperatures based on your daily routines, weather patterns, and even your location. Similarly, smart lighting systems can adjust the brightness and color of lights based on the time of day or activities, creating a more energy-efficient and personalized environment.

Home Security: AI-powered security cameras and smart locks are transforming home security. Devices like Ring and Nest Cam use AI to detect movement, recognize faces, and send real-time alerts to homeowners. They can also integrate with other smart devices to provide a more seamless and automated security experience.

13.2 AI in Entertainment and Media

AI is also revolutionizing the entertainment and media industry by offering more personalized and engaging experiences.

Personalized Recommendations: Streaming platforms like Netflix, Spotify, and YouTube use AI to recommend movies, music, and videos based on your preferences and viewing history. These platforms analyze user behavior and preferences to create customized recommendations, making it easier for users to discover new content tailored to their tastes.

Content Creation: AI is also being used in content creation. In the music industry, AI algorithms can compose music, generate lyrics, and assist in sound mixing. Similarly, in filmmaking, AI can be used to edit videos, generate special effects, and even create realistic CGI characters. These tools help creators work more efficiently and open up new possibilities in the creative process.

Gaming: AI has a significant role in enhancing the gaming experience. Video games use AI to create responsive, intelligent non-playable characters (NPCs) that react to players' actions, making gameplay more immersive. In the future, AI-powered games could adapt to individual players' skills and preferences, offering unique challenges and experiences for each gamer.

13.3 Healthcare at Home

AI-powered healthcare technologies are improving personal well-being and enabling more proactive health management, even from the comfort of home.

Wearables and Health Monitoring: Wearable devices, such as fitness trackers and smartwatches, use AI to monitor vital signs like heart rate, steps taken, and calories burned. These devices can detect irregularities and alert users to potential health issues, prompting early intervention. For example, Apple Watch's ECG feature can detect signs of atrial fibrillation (AFib), a heart condition that often goes undiagnosed.

Telemedicine: Telemedicine platforms, powered by AI, are revolutionizing healthcare delivery by enabling virtual consultations with doctors. AI chatbots can assist patients by answering health-related questions, providing medical advice, and even conducting preliminary diagnostics. This technology is particularly valuable in rural areas or places with limited access to healthcare facilities.

AI in Mental Health: AI-driven mental health apps are helping individuals manage stress, anxiety, and other mental health conditions. These apps use AI to assess users' moods, provide therapeutic exercises, and offer support through virtual counseling sessions. By offering on-demand assistance, AI is making mental health care more accessible and reducing the stigma around seeking help.

13.4 AI in Shopping and Retail

AI is transforming the shopping experience, both online and in physical stores, making it more personalized, convenient, and efficient.

Personalized Shopping Experiences: E-commerce giants like Amazon and Alibaba use AI to analyze customer preferences and shopping behaviors. This data is then used to provide personalized product recommendations, discounts, and offers. AI-powered chatbots also assist customers by answering product-related queries and guiding them through the purchasing process.

Smart Stores and Checkout Systems: In physical retail stores, AI is improving the shopping experience with features like automated checkout systems. For example, Amazon Go stores use AI and computer vision to track items picked up by customers and automatically charge them without the need for checkout lines. Similarly, robots are being used in warehouses to streamline inventory management and order fulfillment.

Virtual Shopping Assistants: AI-powered virtual assistants are being used to provide a more personalized shopping experience. These assistants can help customers find products, compare prices, and even try on clothes virtually using augmented reality (AR). This enhances convenience and allows consumers to make more informed purchasing decisions.

13.5 Transportation and Mobility

AI and automation are also having a significant impact on transportation, making travel safer, more efficient, and more accessible.

Autonomous Vehicles: Self-driving cars and autonomous vehicles are set to revolutionize the transportation industry. These vehicles use AI to navigate roads, avoid obstacles, and make decisions in real-time. Autonomous vehicles could reduce traffic accidents, improve traffic flow, and make transportation more accessible for individuals with disabilities or those unable to drive.

AI in Traffic Management: AI-powered traffic management systems are being implemented in cities to optimize traffic flow and reduce congestion. By analyzing real-time traffic data from sensors and cameras, AI can adjust traffic lights, suggest alternative routes, and provide drivers with real-time traffic updates. This can lead to shorter travel times, reduced fuel consumption, and less pollution.

Ride-Hailing and Mobility Services: Ride-hailing services like Uber and Lyft use AI algorithms to match passengers with nearby drivers, optimize routes, and predict demand. AI is also being used to enhance customer experiences by offering personalized ride recommendations and improving the overall efficiency of these services.

13.6 Ethical Considerations and Privacy Concerns

As AI becomes increasingly embedded in everyday life, there are important ethical and privacy concerns to address. The use of personal data, surveillance, and the potential for bias in AI algorithms raise critical questions about the impact of AI on privacy and civil liberties.

Data Privacy: AI systems often rely on large amounts of personal data to function effectively. However, this data can be vulnerable to breaches, misuse, or unauthorized access. It is essential for companies and governments to implement strong data protection policies to safeguard individuals' privacy and ensure that personal information is used responsibly.

Bias in AI Systems: AI systems are only as good as the data they are trained on. If the data is biased, the resulting algorithms can perpetuate and even amplify these biases. This is a significant concern in areas such as hiring, law enforcement, and lending, where biased AI systems could lead to unfair outcomes. It is crucial to ensure that AI systems are transparent, accountable, and designed to avoid discriminatory practices.

AI and Human Autonomy: As AI takes on more decision-making roles in our lives, there is a growing concern about the loss of human agency. It is important to maintain a balance between the convenience and efficiency offered by AI and the need for human control and decision-making. Ensuring that AI serves as a tool to enhance human life rather than replace it is a key ethical consideration.

13.7 Conclusion: The AI-Powered Future of Everyday Life

AI and automation are already enhancing our daily lives in ways that were once unimaginable. From smarter homes to personalized healthcare, AI is creating more efficient, personalized, and convenient experiences for individuals around the world. As these technologies continue to evolve, we can expect even more profound changes in how we interact with the world around us.

However, as we embrace the benefits of AI, we must also remain vigilant about the ethical, social, and privacy concerns that come with it. By developing AI responsibly and with consideration for its impact on society, we can create a future where AI enhances our lives while safeguarding our rights and values.

Chapter 14: The Role of AI in Business and Industry: Driving Efficiency and Innovation

Artificial Intelligence (AI) and automation are transforming industries across the globe, driving efficiency, reducing costs, and unlocking new opportunities for innovation. As AI technologies become more advanced, their impact on business operations is becoming increasingly profound. In this chapter, we explore how AI is revolutionizing various industries, the key benefits it offers, and the challenges businesses face as they adopt AI-powered solutions.

14.1 AI in Manufacturing: Smart Factories and Automation

AI is playing a crucial role in transforming the manufacturing sector, enabling the creation of smart factories where machines, systems, and processes are interconnected and optimized through AI and automation.

Predictive Maintenance: One of the key benefits of AI in manufacturing is predictive maintenance. AI systems can monitor the performance of machines in real-time, detecting anomalies and predicting when a machine is likely to fail. This allows manufacturers to perform maintenance proactively, minimizing downtime and reducing repair costs.

Supply Chain Optimization: AI is being used to optimize supply chains by forecasting demand, tracking inventory, and improving logistics. Machine learning algorithms analyze historical data and real-time conditions to help businesses make more informed decisions, reducing waste, improving efficiency, and ensuring that products reach customers on time.

Robotics and Automation: Robots powered by AI are increasingly being used in manufacturing to perform repetitive tasks such as assembly, welding, and painting. These robots can work alongside human workers, increasing production speed and improving precision. AI-powered robots can also adapt to changes in the production process, enabling more flexible manufacturing environments.

14.2 AI in Retail: Enhancing Customer Experience and Operations

AI is reshaping the retail industry by enhancing both the customer experience and operational efficiency. Retailers are using AI to personalize shopping experiences, improve inventory management, and streamline supply chains.

Personalized Recommendations: AI-powered recommendation engines, like those used by Amazon and Netflix, are transforming how retailers engage with customers. By analyzing past purchasing behavior and browsing patterns, AI can suggest products tailored to individual preferences, increasing sales and customer satisfaction.

Chatbots and Virtual Assistants: Many retailers are using AI-powered chatbots and virtual assistants to enhance customer service. These AI tools can answer customer queries, assist with product selection, and even handle transactions. By offering 24/7 support, chatbots improve customer experience and reduce the workload of human staff.

Inventory Management: AI is helping retailers manage inventory more efficiently by predicting demand and optimizing stock levels. AI algorithms can analyze sales data and external factors such as weather or local events to predict which products will be in demand. This helps retailers avoid overstocking or running out of popular items.

14.3 AI in Healthcare: Improving Patient Care and Operational Efficiency

The healthcare sector is increasingly turning to AI to enhance patient care, improve operational efficiency, and accelerate medical research. AI has the potential to revolutionize how healthcare is delivered, making it more personalized, accessible, and cost-effective.

Medical Imaging and Diagnostics: AI algorithms are already being used to assist in diagnosing diseases by analyzing medical images such as X-rays, MRIs, and CT scans. These AI tools can identify patterns that might be missed by human doctors, helping to detect conditions such as cancer, heart disease, and neurological disorders at an earlier stage.

Predictive Analytics: AI is being used to predict health outcomes by analyzing large datasets of patient information. For example, AI can analyze electronic health records to predict which patients are at risk for developing certain conditions, enabling doctors to intervene early and prevent complications.

Drug Discovery: AI is speeding up the drug discovery process by analyzing vast amounts of data to identify potential drug candidates. Machine learning algorithms can predict how different compounds will interact with the body, helping researchers identify promising candidates more quickly and accurately.

14.4 AI in Finance: Automating Processes and Enhancing Decision-Making

AI is increasingly being used in the finance industry to automate processes, improve risk management, and enhance decision-making. From automated trading systems to fraud detection, AI is reshaping the financial landscape.

Algorithmic Trading: AI-powered algorithms are used in stock trading to analyze vast amounts of market data and make trading decisions in real-time. These algorithms can identify patterns and trends that humans might miss, allowing traders to make more informed decisions and execute trades faster than ever before.

Fraud Detection and Prevention: AI is being used to detect fraudulent activities in financial transactions by analyzing patterns and identifying anomalies. Machine learning algorithms can flag suspicious transactions in real-time, allowing banks and financial institutions to take immediate action to prevent fraud.

Credit Scoring and Risk Management: AI is improving the accuracy of credit scoring models by analyzing a broader range of data, including non-traditional factors like social media activity and transaction history. This allows financial institutions to make more accurate predictions about an individual's creditworthiness, enabling better decision-making and reducing risk.

14.5 AI in Marketing: Targeted Campaigns and Consumer Insights

AI is transforming the marketing industry by enabling businesses to deliver more personalized, targeted, and effective marketing campaigns. By analyzing consumer data and behavior, AI helps marketers understand their audiences better and tailor their messages accordingly.

Customer Segmentation: AI algorithms can analyze customer data to segment audiences based on factors like demographics, purchase behavior, and preferences. This allows marketers to target specific groups with personalized offers, increasing the likelihood of conversion and improving return on investment.

Predictive Analytics: AI is helping businesses predict consumer behavior and trends by analyzing historical data. Marketers can use AI to anticipate what products or services customers are likely to purchase, allowing them to create more effective campaigns and optimize their marketing budgets.

Content Creation: AI tools are being used to generate content for marketing campaigns. From writing product descriptions to creating social media posts,

AI-powered content generation tools can save time and resources while ensuring that content is engaging and relevant to the target audience.

14.6 AI in Logistics and Supply Chain Management

The logistics and supply chain industry is leveraging AI to streamline operations, reduce costs, and improve delivery times. AI is helping companies optimize routes, track shipments, and manage inventory more efficiently.

Route Optimization: AI algorithms are used to optimize delivery routes by analyzing traffic patterns, weather conditions, and other variables. This helps logistics companies reduce fuel costs, minimize delays, and improve delivery efficiency.

Autonomous Vehicles and Drones: Autonomous trucks and drones powered by AI are being used to transport goods more efficiently. These vehicles can navigate roads and airspace without human intervention, reducing transportation costs and improving delivery speeds.

Supply Chain Visibility: AI is improving visibility in the supply chain by tracking shipments in real-time. This allows businesses to monitor the progress of their deliveries, identify potential delays, and take corrective action before problems arise.

14.7 Challenges in Implementing AI in Business

While AI offers numerous benefits to businesses, its adoption comes with challenges that must be addressed. These challenges include:

High Implementation Costs: Implementing AI solutions can be expensive, particularly for small and medium-sized businesses. The cost of developing, deploying, and maintaining AI systems can be a barrier to adoption for many companies.

Data Privacy and Security: As AI systems rely on large amounts of data to function, businesses must ensure that they protect customer and employee data from breaches and misuse. Implementing robust data security measures is critical to maintaining trust and compliance with regulations.

Lack of Skilled Workforce: The adoption of AI requires specialized knowledge and skills, which are in high demand. Businesses may struggle to find employees with the necessary expertise to develop and manage AI systems, making workforce training and recruitment an ongoing challenge.

Ethical and Bias Concerns: AI systems can inadvertently perpetuate biases if they are trained on biased data. Businesses must ensure that their AI systems are fair, transparent, and ethical, particularly in areas like hiring, lending, and customer service.

14.8 Conclusion: Embracing AI for Business Success

AI and automation are reshaping the way businesses operate, offering significant opportunities for increased efficiency, reduced costs, and enhanced innovation. While challenges exist, the potential benefits far outweigh the risks. By embracing AI and investing in the right tools and talent, businesses can unlock new growth opportunities, improve customer experiences, and stay competitive in an increasingly automated world.

As AI continues to evolve, businesses that successfully integrate these technologies into their operations will be well-positioned to thrive in the future. The key to success lies in leveraging AI responsibly, ensuring ethical practices, and continuously adapting to the changing landscape of technology.

Chapter 15: AI in Education: Transforming Learning and Teaching

The educational sector is increasingly embracing artificial intelligence (AI) to improve both learning experiences and administrative processes. From personalized learning paths to AI-driven tutoring systems, AI has the potential to revolutionize education, making it more accessible, efficient, and tailored to individual needs.

15.1 Personalized Learning: Customizing Education for Every Student

One of the most significant advantages of AI in education is its ability to provide personalized learning experiences. AI systems can analyze students' learning styles, strengths, and weaknesses, and then adapt educational content to suit their needs.

Adaptive Learning Platforms: AI-driven adaptive learning platforms adjust the difficulty of tasks and the type of content presented based on the learner's progress. For instance, if a student struggles with a particular topic, the system can provide additional exercises or simpler explanations to reinforce the concept before moving on to more advanced material.

Learning Analytics: AI can track student performance over time and identify areas where they need additional help. Teachers can use this data to create targeted interventions, ensuring that no student falls behind and each one receives the support they need to succeed.

15.2 AI-Powered Tutoring Systems

AI-powered tutoring systems are becoming increasingly popular in the education sector, providing students with access to personalized, on-demand learning support. These systems use natural language processing (NLP) and machine learning to simulate human tutoring.

24/7 Assistance: AI-based tutors are available at all hours, offering instant help with homework, assignments, or subject-related queries. This allows students to learn at their own pace and seek help whenever they need it, even outside of regular school hours.

Instant Feedback: Unlike traditional methods, where feedback might take time to reach students, AI tutors provide immediate responses to students' queries. This instant feedback helps students correct mistakes and reinforce their learning in real-time.

15.3 Automating Administrative Tasks

AI is also streamlining administrative tasks in schools and universities, allowing educators to spend more time focusing on teaching and less on paperwork.

Grading and Assessments: AI can automate the grading process, particularly for objective assignments like multiple-choice questions, essays, and problem-solving tasks. This not only saves time but also ensures consistency and fairness in grading.

Administrative Assistance: AI systems can handle administrative tasks such as scheduling, record-keeping, and student enrollment, improving efficiency and reducing the administrative burden on staff. This frees up resources for other critical areas of the educational process.

15.4 AI in Special Education: Bridging the Gap

AI is playing a significant role in making education more inclusive for students with disabilities. Through various applications, AI is helping to provide specialized support for students with learning differences.

Assistive Technologies: AI-powered tools such as speech recognition software, text-to-speech applications, and communication aids are helping students with disabilities engage in the learning process. These technologies can assist students with hearing impairments, visual impairments, and learning disabilities, allowing them to participate in classroom activities and improve their learning outcomes.

Personalized Learning for Special Needs: AI-driven platforms are being developed to cater specifically to students with special needs, offering tailored lessons and feedback that address their individual learning styles and abilities. This ensures that all students, regardless of their challenges, can receive a high-quality education.

15.5 AI in Language Learning

AI is also transforming the way languages are taught and learned. Through the use of speech recognition, natural language processing, and other AI technologies, students can practice speaking and writing in different languages more effectively.

Speech Recognition and Pronunciation Assistance: AI-powered apps and tools can assess students' pronunciation and provide instant feedback. These systems can identify mistakes, offer suggestions for improvement, and help learners become more confident in speaking foreign languages.

Interactive Language Learning Platforms: AI-driven language learning platforms, like Duolingo and Babbel, use machine learning to personalize lessons based on a learner's progress and language proficiency. These platforms engage students in interactive exercises, making language learning more fun and effective.

15.6 AI in Assessment and Evaluation

AI is improving the way we assess students' learning and progress. Traditional assessment methods often focus on testing rote memorization and basic understanding, but AI enables more dynamic and comprehensive evaluation.

Dynamic Assessments: AI-based assessment tools can test students' problem-solving abilities, critical thinking skills, and creativity. These assessments adapt based on the learner's performance and provide a more accurate picture of their overall abilities.

Predictive Analytics: AI can analyze student performance over time and predict future academic success. These insights can help educators intervene early when students are at risk of falling behind or not meeting learning goals.

15.7 Challenges of AI in Education

While AI offers many advantages, its integration into education also comes with challenges that need to be addressed.

Data Privacy Concerns: AI systems in education rely on large amounts of student data, which raises concerns about data privacy and security. Ensuring that student data is protected from breaches and misuse is critical to maintaining trust and compliance with regulations.

Equity in Access: Not all students have equal access to AI-powered educational tools. Disparities in technology access, particularly in rural or underprivileged areas, could exacerbate educational inequalities. Ensuring that AI technologies are accessible to all students is a key challenge for educators and policymakers.

Teacher Training: For AI to be effectively integrated into the classroom, teachers need to be trained in how to use these technologies. Without adequate professional development and support, educators may struggle to incorporate AI into their teaching practices.

Ethical Issues: The use of AI in education raises ethical concerns regarding bias, fairness, and the role of technology in shaping students' educational experiences. It's essential that AI tools are developed and implemented in ways that are fair, transparent, and aligned with ethical principles.

15.8 The Future of AI in Education

The future of AI in education looks promising, with continued advancements in AI technology set to further enhance learning and teaching experiences. As AI becomes more sophisticated, it will play an even more significant role in creating personalized, accessible, and effective education systems.

Lifelong Learning: AI will support lifelong learning by providing learners with customized learning experiences throughout their lives. Whether someone is acquiring new skills for career development or pursuing personal interests, AI can provide the tools and resources needed for continuous learning.

AI-Enhanced Teaching: Teachers will have access to AI tools that can help them design more effective lessons, track student progress, and provide personalized support. AI will not replace teachers but will complement their efforts by enhancing their ability to meet the needs of diverse learners.

Global Education Systems: AI has the potential to break down geographical and cultural barriers to education. With the rise of online learning platforms, AI can provide quality education to students anywhere in the world, making education more equitable and accessible.

15.9 Conclusion: The Transformative Power of AI in Education

AI is poised to reshape the educational landscape, offering new ways to engage students, support teachers, and improve learning outcomes. By harnessing the power of AI, education systems can become more personalized, inclusive, and efficient. However, as with any new technology, it is important to approach AI in education thoughtfully, ensuring that its implementation is ethical, equitable, and beneficial for all learners.

As we look to the future, AI's potential to revolutionize education is immense. By embracing these technologies and addressing the challenges they present, we can unlock a brighter, more innovative future for students and educators worldwide.

Chapter 16: AI in Creative Industries: Art, Music, and Design

Artificial Intelligence (AI) is rapidly transforming creative industries such as art, music, and design. Traditionally, these fields relied on human intuition, skill, and expression to create meaningful works. However, AI has introduced new possibilities for collaboration between human creativity and machine learning, enabling artists, musicians, and designers to explore innovative forms of expression and push the boundaries of traditional mediums.

16.1 AI in Visual Arts: Redefining Creativity

AI has had a profound impact on the world of visual arts, enabling artists to create unique and complex works that were previously unimaginable. AI can analyze thousands of images, patterns, and styles to generate new works of art, offering a fusion of artistic tradition and cutting-edge technology.

Generative Art: AI algorithms, like Generative Adversarial Networks (GANs), are capable of producing artwork that mimics the style of famous artists or invents entirely new aesthetics. These AI-generated pieces challenge traditional notions of authorship and creativity, prompting important discussions about the role of machines in art creation.

Collaborative Art: Many contemporary artists now use AI as a tool to collaborate with machines in their creative process. By providing the AI with input or parameters, artists can guide the machine's artistic choices while still retaining their own creative vision. This collaboration between human and machine offers endless possibilities for new forms of art.

Art Preservation: AI is also playing a role in art preservation by helping to restore old and damaged artworks. Machine learning algorithms can analyze paintings and sculptures, identifying areas that need restoration and providing suggestions on how to bring them back to their original state.

16.2 AI in Music: Composing the Future

Music composition has long been seen as a domain of human creativity, but AI is now stepping in to assist musicians in composing melodies, harmonies, and entire symphonies. AI tools for music generation use machine learning models trained on vast databases of musical compositions to produce new pieces of music that adhere to specific genres, styles, and structures.

AI Music Composers: Tools like OpenAI's MuseNet and Sony's Flow Machines are capable of composing original music across a wide variety of genres, from classical to contemporary pop. These AI systems can analyze patterns in existing music and generate compositions that reflect these patterns, offering musicians new sources of inspiration and creative ideas.

Personalized Music: AI is being used to create personalized music experiences for listeners. AI-driven music platforms, like Spotify's recommendation engine, analyze user preferences and listening habits to curate playlists and suggest new tracks. This ability to tailor music to an individual's tastes has changed the way people discover and engage with music.

AI-Assisted Music Production: Musicians are using AI to streamline the music production process. AI tools can help with tasks such as mixing, mastering, and sound design, making it easier for artists to create high-quality tracks without needing a professional studio. These tools can also help with musical experimentation, suggesting new combinations of sounds and styles.

16.4 AI in Architecture and Interior Design:

Shaping the Future of Spaces

AI is making waves in architecture and interior design by offering tools for creating more efficient, aesthetically pleasing, and sustainable structures. Architects and designers can use AI to optimize designs, analyze building performance, and even predict how a space will function in the future.

Generative Design in Architecture: AI-powered generative design tools can create a variety of design options based on specific parameters, such as material efficiency, aesthetic preferences, and environmental impact. Architects can input their goals into the system, and the AI will generate multiple designs, helping them to explore new possibilities and make more informed design decisions.

Smart Buildings and Interior Design: AI is also contributing to the rise of smart buildings and homes. Through the use of sensors, AI systems can control lighting, heating, and cooling based on occupancy patterns and environmental conditions. In interior design, AI is helping to create personalized spaces by analyzing users' preferences and behaviors, suggesting layouts, furniture, and decor that align with their tastes.

Sustainability and Efficiency: Just as in fashion, AI in architecture helps optimize for sustainability. By using AI to model energy consumption and material use, architects can design buildings that are more energy-efficient and environmentally friendly. These technologies are essential as the world moves toward greener, more sustainable construction practices.

16.5 The Impact of AI on Creative Collaboration

AI is reshaping how creative professionals collaborate with each other, enabling cross-disciplinary teamwork and offering new tools for collaboration that were once unimaginable.

Interdisciplinary Collaboration: Artists, musicians, designers, and engineers are increasingly working together on projects where AI is at the core. For example, musicians and software developers collaborate to create AI tools that can generate music, while artists and computer scientists work on AI-driven art installations. These cross-disciplinary partnerships open up new avenues for creativity and innovation.

Crowdsourced Creativity: AI also enables crowdsourced creativity, where people from different backgrounds contribute to a shared creative project. AI systems can analyze and combine input from a diverse range of individuals, creating something that none of the participants could have envisioned on their own.

AI as a Co-Creator: Rather than replacing human artists, AI is acting as a co-creator, offering new ideas, enhancing creativity, and assisting in the execution of complex tasks. This partnership between humans and machines is redefining the creative process, allowing for the creation of more diverse and experimental works of art.

16.6 Challenges and Ethical Considerations

Despite the many opportunities AI presents in creative industries, its integration also raises several ethical and practical challenges.

Intellectual Property Issues: The rise of AI-generated art and music raises questions about ownership and authorship. Who owns the rights to a piece of art created by an AI? Should AI-generated works be credited to the developers of the AI or to the machine itself? These are complex questions that the creative industries must address.

Creativity vs. Automation: While AI can produce remarkable works of art and music, there are concerns that over-reliance on AI could lead to the loss of human creativity. Will AI become a crutch for creators, or will it inspire new forms of expression? Balancing the benefits of AI with the need to preserve human creativity is a key challenge.

Bias in AI-Generated Content: AI systems are only as good as the data they are trained on. If the data contains biases—whether cultural, racial, or gender-based—these biases can be reflected in the AI-generated content. This is a significant concern in creative industries, where diversity and inclusivity are crucial.

16.7 The Future of AI in Creative Industries

As AI continues to evolve, its role in creative industries will only grow. The future holds exciting possibilities for how AI can collaborate with human creators to produce works that challenge our understanding of art, music, and design.

Immersive Experiences: With advancements in virtual reality (VR) and augmented reality (AR), AI is poised to create immersive art and music experiences that engage multiple senses. These experiences will not only be interactive but will also evolve in real-time, based on user input and AI-generated content.

AI-Powered Creativity Platforms: In the future, AI-driven platforms may become commonplace, allowing creators of all levels to collaborate with AI tools to produce high-quality work. These platforms will democratize creativity, enabling anyone to create professional-level art, music, or design with the help of AI.

16.8 Conclusion: AI and the Boundaries of Creativity

AI has already made a significant impact on creative industries, and its potential to reshape art, music, and design is vast. As AI continues to advance, it will open up new opportunities for collaboration, innovation, and creativity. Rather than replacing human artists, AI is enhancing their capabilities and offering new ways to express ideas and emotions.

By working alongside AI, creators are not only producing groundbreaking work but also exploring the very nature of creativity itself. As we move into the future, AI's role in creative industries will continue to evolve, pushing the boundaries of what is possible and redefining the intersection between art and technology.

Chapter 17: The Ethics of AI: Balancing Innovation and Responsibility

As Artificial Intelligence (AI) becomes more integrated into various sectors, the ethical implications of its use have come under intense scrutiny. While AI offers immense potential for innovation, it also raises several challenges concerning fairness, transparency, accountability, and societal impact. In this chapter, we will explore the ethical concerns surrounding AI, the challenges in maintaining a balance between progress and responsibility, and the steps being taken to ensure that AI benefits humanity as a whole.

17.1 The Need for Ethical Frameworks in AI

AI technologies have the ability to affect nearly every aspect of human life, from healthcare and education to employment and privacy. This widespread influence makes it crucial to establish clear ethical guidelines to govern AI development and usage. Without these frameworks, AI has the potential to cause harm, intentionally or unintentionally, due to biases, lack of accountability, or misuse.

Establishing Ethical Standards: Several organizations, including governments and independent research groups, are working on creating ethical standards for AI. These standards focus on transparency, ensuring that AI systems make decisions that are understandable and explainable to the public. Ethical AI also emphasizes accountability, making sure that human stakeholders are responsible for the actions of AI systems.

AI and Human Rights: One of the key ethical concerns is ensuring that AI systems respect human rights, such as the right to privacy, freedom of speech, and non-discrimination. As AI systems become more autonomous, there is a risk that they could infringe upon individual rights without proper oversight. Ensuring that AI operates within the bounds of these rights is a critical consideration for its ethical implementation.

17.2 Bias and Discrimination in AI

AI systems, particularly those driven by machine learning, rely heavily on large datasets to make decisions. However, these datasets can sometimes contain biases that reflect societal inequalities. If AI systems are trained on biased data, they can reproduce and even amplify these biases, leading to unfair outcomes.

Algorithmic Bias: One of the most significant concerns is that AI systems can perpetuate biases based on race, gender, age, or other characteristics. For example, facial recognition technologies have been shown to have higher error rates for people of color, leading to concerns about their use in law enforcement. Similarly, AI used in hiring processes can unintentionally discriminate against women or minority groups if trained on biased historical data.

Mitigating Bias: Addressing bias in AI involves creating more diverse and representative datasets, along with designing algorithms that can identify and correct bias. Companies and research institutions are actively working on developing techniques to reduce bias in AI systems, but it remains a challenging issue that requires ongoing attention.

17.3 AI and Job Displacement: Ethical Considerations

One of the most significant societal impacts of AI is its potential to displace human workers in various industries. As automation and AI-driven technologies become more advanced, many jobs that were once performed by humans are now being done by machines. This raises several ethical questions:

Job Loss and Economic Inequality: While AI can increase productivity and create new industries, it also poses a threat to jobs in fields like manufacturing, retail, and even knowledge work. The displacement of workers can exacerbate economic inequality, as workers in low-skill jobs may find it more difficult to transition to new roles that require advanced technical skills.

Ensuring Fair Transition: Ethical considerations around job displacement call for policies that ensure workers are supported during transitions. Governments and businesses must invest in upskilling and reskilling programs to help workers adapt to the changing job market. Additionally, universal basic income (UBI) and other safety nets are being proposed as solutions to mitigate the financial impact on displaced workers.

17.4 Transparency and Accountability in AI Decision-Making

AI systems are increasingly being used to make important decisions that affect individuals and society, such as in hiring, law enforcement, credit scoring, and healthcare. However, many AI algorithms are complex and operate as "black boxes," meaning that their decision-making processes are not transparent or easily understood by humans.

The Black Box Problem: The lack of transparency in AI systems leads to concerns about accountability. If an AI system makes a decision that negatively affects an individual, it can be difficult to determine why the decision was made or who is responsible for the outcome. This lack of explainability can erode trust in AI systems and create risks for users.

Explainable AI (XAI): Efforts are being made to develop explainable AI, which focuses on creating models whose decisions are transparent and understandable. By ensuring that AI systems can explain their reasoning, we can increase trust in their use and make it easier to hold the relevant parties accountable for their actions.

17.5 AI and Privacy Concerns

As AI systems process vast amounts of personal data to function effectively, privacy concerns have become a major issue. AI technologies such as facial recognition, surveillance systems, and data analytics can potentially infringe on individuals' privacy rights if not properly regulated.

Data Privacy: AI systems rely on personal data to learn and make decisions. However, if this data is not securely stored and managed, it can be accessed and misused by unauthorized parties. In addition, individuals may not always be aware of how their data is being used or whether it is being used in ways that violate their privacy.

Surveillance and Control: The use of AI in surveillance systems raises concerns about governmental overreach and the potential for control over personal freedoms. AI-powered surveillance cameras and data collection tools could enable governments or corporations to monitor individuals on an unprecedented scale, which could have serious consequences for civil liberties.

Ensuring Privacy Protection: Ethical AI development includes ensuring that personal data is protected and used responsibly. This can be achieved through data encryption, anonymization, and strict data governance policies. Additionally, individuals should have more control over their own data, including the ability to opt out of data collection processes.

17.6 The Role of AI in Autonomous Weapons

One of the most controversial ethical issues surrounding AI is its application in autonomous weapons systems. These are AI-powered machines capable of making decisions about targeting and engaging with enemy forces without human intervention. The development and deployment of autonomous weapons raise significant ethical concerns:

Loss of Human Control: The main concern is that autonomous weapons could make life-and-death decisions without human oversight, leading to potential misuse or unintended consequences. These systems could potentially be hacked or malfunction, causing harm to innocent people.

Accountability in Warfare: If an autonomous weapon system causes civilian casualties, determining accountability becomes a complex issue. Should the developers of the system be held responsible? What about the military commanders who deploy the system? These questions pose major ethical challenges in the use of AI in warfare.

International Regulation: Many experts and organizations are calling for international regulations on the development and use of autonomous weapons. The goal is to ensure that AI-driven military technologies do not lead to an arms race or undermine international peace and security.

17.7 AI and Environmental Impact

While AI holds great potential to improve sustainability, there are also concerns about its environmental impact. The energy consumption of AI systems, particularly deep learning models, is a growing concern, as these systems require significant computational power and resources.

Energy Consumption: Training large AI models involves the use of high-performance computing resources, which consume a considerable amount of energy. This energy consumption contributes to the carbon footprint of AI technologies, raising questions about their long-term environmental sustainability.

AI for Sustainability: On the positive side, AI can also be used to promote environmental sustainability. AI systems are being deployed in various sectors, such as energy management, climate modeling, and waste reduction, to optimize resource use and reduce environmental damage. The ethical challenge lies in balancing AI's environmental costs with its potential to address global sustainability issues.

17.8 The Future of AI Ethics

As AI continues to evolve, it is imperative that its ethical considerations evolve alongside it. The future of AI ethics will likely involve ongoing debates about how to balance innovation with responsibility, ensuring that AI technologies benefit humanity without causing harm.

Global Collaboration: AI ethics is a global issue that requires collaboration between governments, industry leaders, and researchers. Creating international agreements and regulations will be key to ensuring that AI is developed and deployed responsibly, taking into account the diverse needs and values of different cultures.

Continuous Monitoring: Ethical AI development is not a one-time task but an ongoing process. Continuous monitoring and evaluation of AI systems are necessary to identify potential issues, address new challenges, and ensure that AI remains aligned with human values.

17.9 Conclusion: Navigating the Ethical Landscape of AI

As AI becomes an integral part of our world, it is crucial to address the ethical concerns that accompany its development. By creating robust ethical frameworks, promoting transparency, and ensuring accountability, we can harness the power of AI while minimizing its risks. The goal should be to create AI systems that not only enhance human life but also respect fundamental ethical principles and values.

The future of AI is full of promise, but it is essential that we proceed with caution and responsibility. By doing so, we can ensure that AI serves as a force for good, driving progress while safeguarding the well-being of individuals and society as a whole.

Chapter 18: AI in Healthcare: Revolutionizing Medicine

Artificial Intelligence (AI) has the potential to revolutionize healthcare by improving diagnosis, treatment, and patient outcomes. As AI systems become more advanced, they are increasingly being integrated into healthcare settings, from hospitals to research labs, offering groundbreaking solutions to complex medical challenges. In this chapter, we will explore the transformative impact of AI in healthcare, its applications, benefits, challenges, and the ethical considerations associated with its use.

18.1 AI in Medical Diagnosis

One of the most significant areas where AI is making an impact is in medical diagnosis. AI algorithms, especially those powered by machine learning and deep learning, are being used to analyze medical data, identify patterns, and assist doctors in diagnosing diseases more accurately and efficiently.

Medical Imaging: AI systems are being used to analyze medical images, such as X-rays, CT scans, and MRIs, to detect conditions like cancer, heart disease, and neurological disorders. These systems can often identify abnormalities with greater accuracy than human doctors, especially in the early stages of disease, leading to quicker diagnoses and better outcomes.

Predictive Diagnostics: AI can also analyze patient data to predict the likelihood of developing certain conditions. For example, AI-powered tools can predict the risk of heart disease, diabetes, or even mental health conditions based on patient history, genetics, and lifestyle factors. This predictive capability allows healthcare providers to intervene earlier and take preventive measures, improving long-term health outcomes.

18.2 AI in Personalized Medicine

Personalized medicine, or precision medicine, is an approach that tailors medical treatment to the individual characteristics of each patient. AI plays a crucial role in advancing personalized medicine by analyzing vast amounts of data to identify the most effective treatments for specific patients based on their genetic makeup, lifestyle, and medical history.

Genomic Analysis: AI systems are increasingly being used in genomics to analyze DNA sequences and identify genetic variations that may predispose individuals to certain diseases. By understanding a patient's genetic profile, doctors can develop personalized treatment plans, selecting the most effective drugs and therapies for that individual.

Drug Development: AI is also transforming drug discovery and development. Traditional drug discovery is a time-consuming and expensive process, but AI can analyze large datasets to identify potential drug candidates, predict their effectiveness, and speed up the development process. AI is already being used to identify new treatments for diseases like cancer, Alzheimer's, and COVID-19.

18.3 AI in Surgery: Enhancing Precision and Minimizing Risk

AI is increasingly being used in the operating room to assist surgeons and improve the precision of surgical procedures. Robotic surgery, powered by AI, is becoming more common, allowing for minimally invasive procedures that reduce the risk of complications and speed up recovery times for patients.

Robotic-Assisted Surgery: AI-powered robotic systems, such as the da Vinci Surgical System, allow surgeons to perform complex procedures with greater precision. These systems can assist in tasks such as making incisions, suturing, and navigating delicate structures, all while minimizing the risk of human error.

Surgical Planning and Simulation: AI can also assist in planning surgeries by analyzing patient data, such as medical images and records, to create customized surgical plans. Additionally, AI-driven simulation tools can help surgeons practice procedures in a virtual environment, improving their skills and reducing the risk of complications during real surgeries.

18.4 AI in Drug Discovery and Clinical Trials

The development of new drugs and treatments is a lengthy process that requires extensive research and clinical trials. AI is helping to streamline this process by analyzing data from previous studies, identifying potential drug candidates, and even designing clinical trials that are more likely to succeed.

Accelerating Drug Discovery: AI can rapidly analyze vast amounts of biomedical data to identify potential drug compounds that may have therapeutic effects. For example, AI can identify existing drugs that might be repurposed for new diseases, saving both time and resources in drug development.

Optimizing Clinical Trials: AI is also transforming the way clinical trials are conducted. By analyzing patient data, AI can help identify the most suitable candidates for clinical trials, ensuring that trials are more focused and have higher success rates. Additionally, AI can monitor trial progress in real time, identifying potential issues early and making adjustments to improve outcomes.

18.5 AI in Healthcare Administration

AI is also playing a significant role in improving the efficiency and effectiveness of healthcare administration. By automating repetitive tasks, optimizing resource allocation, and streamlining workflows, AI helps healthcare providers focus more on patient care and less on administrative duties.

Automating Administrative Tasks: AI-powered systems are being used to automate tasks such as scheduling, billing, and patient record management. These systems reduce the administrative burden on healthcare professionals and improve the overall efficiency of healthcare facilities.

Optimizing Healthcare Operations: AI can analyze hospital data to optimize resource allocation, such as managing the availability of hospital beds, equipment, and medical staff. By predicting patient flow and demand, AI helps hospitals ensure that they are well-prepared for any influx of patients, improving patient care and operational efficiency.

18.6 AI in Mental Health

AI is also being used to improve mental health care by providing personalized treatment plans, identifying at-risk individuals, and offering virtual therapy solutions.

Predicting Mental Health Issues: AI systems can analyze patterns in speech, behavior, and social media activity to predict mental health issues such as depression, anxiety, and schizophrenia. By identifying early warning signs, AI can help healthcare providers intervene sooner and provide appropriate care.

Virtual Therapy: AI-powered chatbots and virtual assistants are being used to provide cognitive behavioral therapy (CBT) and other therapeutic interventions. These AI-driven systems offer accessible and affordable mental health support, especially for individuals who may not have access to traditional therapy.

18.7 Ethical Considerations in AI-Driven Healthcare

While AI offers many potential benefits in healthcare, it also raises several ethical concerns. The use of AI in medicine must be approached with caution to ensure that it is used responsibly and fairly.

Data Privacy: AI systems rely on vast amounts of patient data, raising concerns about data privacy and security. Protecting patient data is crucial to maintaining trust in AI-driven healthcare solutions. Healthcare providers must ensure that patient data is securely stored and only used for legitimate purposes.

Bias and Discrimination: AI systems can perpetuate biases present in the data they are trained on. If AI algorithms are trained on biased data, they may produce skewed results that disproportionately affect certain groups of people. Ensuring that AI systems are trained on diverse and representative datasets is essential to avoid discrimination.

Accountability: When AI systems are involved in medical decisions, determining accountability can be challenging. If an AI system makes an error that harms a patient, it is important to establish who is responsible for the decision—whether it's the healthcare provider, the developers of the AI system, or the AI itself.

18.8 The Future of AI in Healthcare

The future of AI in healthcare is promising, with the potential to greatly improve patient outcomes, reduce costs, and increase access to healthcare services. As AI technologies continue to evolve, they will likely play an even greater role in shaping the healthcare landscape.

AI-Driven Health Monitoring: In the future, AI may be used to continuously monitor patients' health through wearable devices, allowing for real-time data collection and analysis. These systems could detect early signs of disease and alert healthcare providers before symptoms become severe.

Integrating AI with Other Technologies: The integration of AI with other emerging technologies, such as the Internet of Things (IoT) and blockchain, could further enhance the healthcare industry. For example, AI could be used to analyze data from IoT devices, providing healthcare providers with real-time insights into patients' conditions and improving decision-making.

18.9 Conclusion: AI's Impact on Healthcare

AI has the potential to revolutionize healthcare by improving diagnosis, personalizing treatment, enhancing surgical precision, and making healthcare more efficient. While there are challenges and ethical concerns, the benefits of AI in healthcare are undeniable. As technology continues to advance, AI will likely become an even more integral part of the healthcare system, ultimately improving patient care and outcomes.

The future of AI in healthcare looks bright, with innovations that will drive progress in the fight against disease, improve patient experiences, and enhance the overall quality of care.

Chapter 19: AI in Business: Transforming the Corporate World

Artificial Intelligence (AI) is not just a tool for scientific research or healthcare; it is also transforming the business world. From customer service to data analytics, AI is revolutionizing how businesses operate, making processes more efficient, reducing costs, and improving customer experiences. In this chapter, we will explore how AI is being used across various industries, its impact on business models, and the future possibilities it offers for organizations worldwide.

19.1 AI in Customer Service

One of the most widespread applications of AI in business is in customer service. Companies are increasingly turning to AI-powered chatbots, virtual assistants, and automated systems to handle customer queries, complaints, and requests. These AI tools not only improve efficiency but also enhance customer satisfaction by providing 24/7 support and immediate responses.

Chatbots and Virtual Assistants: AI-driven chatbots are capable of handling a wide range of customer inquiries without human intervention. These chatbots can understand natural language, resolve issues, recommend products, and even help with transactions. Virtual assistants, such as Siri, Alexa, or Google Assistant, are also becoming more integrated into business customer support systems, providing personalized assistance to users.

Automated Customer Support: Beyond chatbots, AI is being used in call centers to handle customer inquiries through voice recognition and natural language processing (NLP). These systems can analyze the sentiment of a customer's voice and respond accordingly, offering more personalized and effective support.

19.2 AI in Data Analytics

Data is one of the most valuable assets for any business, and AI is helping organizations unlock the full potential of their data. By utilizing machine learning algorithms, businesses can extract insights from large datasets, identify trends, predict outcomes, and make data-driven decisions.

Predictive Analytics: AI algorithms can analyze historical data to predict future trends. This can be applied in various business sectors, such as forecasting sales, identifying market trends, and predicting customer behavior. Predictive analytics helps businesses stay ahead of the competition and adapt to market changes quickly.

Customer Insights: AI helps companies better understand their customers by analyzing purchasing behavior, preferences, and feedback. This enables businesses to personalize their marketing strategies, optimize pricing, and create targeted campaigns that resonate with their customers.

19.3 AI in Marketing and Sales

AI is transforming marketing and sales strategies by providing businesses with the tools to better understand their customers and reach them through personalized campaigns. Through AI-driven insights, companies can optimize their advertising strategies, improve conversion rates, and increase customer engagement.

Personalized Marketing: AI can analyze customer data to create personalized marketing content, whether it's through emails, ads, or website content. By understanding customer preferences, AI can deliver targeted messages that are more likely to convert into sales.

Sales Forecasting: AI can predict sales trends based on historical data and customer behavior. This allows businesses to optimize their sales strategies and ensure they meet customer demand. AI-powered tools can also help identify the best sales leads, streamlining the sales process and improving conversion rates.

19.4 AI in Supply Chain Management

AI is increasingly being used to optimize supply chain operations, from inventory management to logistics. By automating processes, predicting demand, and analyzing supply chain data, AI helps businesses reduce costs, improve efficiency, and ensure timely deliveries.

Demand Forecasting: AI systems can predict customer demand by analyzing historical sales data, seasonal trends, and market conditions. This allows businesses to optimize inventory levels, avoid stockouts, and reduce excess inventory, leading to significant cost savings.

Route Optimization and Logistics: AI-powered tools are used to optimize delivery routes for goods, reducing transportation costs and improving delivery speed. AI can analyze traffic patterns, weather conditions, and customer preferences to determine the most efficient routes for delivery trucks.

19.5 AI in Human Resources

Human resources (HR) departments are leveraging AI to streamline recruitment, improve employee engagement, and enhance productivity. AI is being used to automate repetitive HR tasks, such as screening resumes and scheduling interviews, allowing HR professionals to focus on more strategic activities.

Recruitment and Hiring: AI can analyze resumes and job applications to identify the best candidates based on specific criteria. This helps companies save time and resources during the hiring process, ensuring they select the most qualified candidates for the job. AI tools can also conduct initial interviews, assess candidates' skills, and predict how well they might perform in the role.

Employee Engagement: AI can be used to monitor employee satisfaction and performance, providing insights into how engaged employees are. By analyzing feedback from surveys, performance reviews, and employee interactions, AI can help HR departments address issues related to employee morale and retention.

19.6 AI in Financial Services

The financial industry is one of the earliest adopters of AI, utilizing it for a wide range of applications, from fraud detection to risk assessment and customer service. AI is helping financial institutions enhance security, improve decision-making, and offer personalized services to their clients.

Fraud Detection and Prevention: AI systems are capable of analyzing vast amounts of transaction data in real-time to detect unusual patterns that may indicate fraud. These systems can identify potential fraudulent activity faster than traditional methods, reducing the risk of financial loss.

Credit Scoring and Risk Assessment: AI is used by financial institutions to assess creditworthiness by analyzing factors such as a person's financial history, payment patterns, and even social behavior. AI-powered credit scoring models are more accurate and inclusive than traditional methods, allowing lenders to make better decisions.

Chatbots in Banking: Many banks are using AI-powered chatbots to assist customers with routine banking tasks, such as checking account balances, transferring funds, and paying bills. These chatbots provide instant support, improving the customer experience and reducing the need for human intervention.

19.7 AI in Retail

AI is revolutionizing the retail industry by enhancing customer experiences, optimizing inventory management, and improving pricing strategies. Retailers are increasingly relying on AI to create personalized shopping experiences and streamline their operations.

Personalized Shopping Experience: AI systems analyze customer behavior to offer personalized product recommendations. For example, e-commerce websites use AI to suggest products based on a customer's browsing history, purchase behavior, and preferences, increasing the likelihood of a sale.

Dynamic Pricing: AI is being used to adjust pricing in real-time based on factors such as demand, competitor prices, and inventory levels. Dynamic pricing allows retailers to remain competitive while maximizing their profits.

Inventory Management: AI-powered systems help retailers manage inventory by predicting demand, optimizing stock levels, and reducing waste. These systems can also help prevent stockouts by ensuring that products are always available when customers need them.

19.8 AI in Manufacturing

AI is transforming the manufacturing industry by improving production efficiency, reducing downtime, and ensuring higher product quality. AI-driven automation is streamlining manufacturing processes, while predictive maintenance helps to prevent costly machine failures.

Predictive Maintenance: AI-powered systems can predict when a machine is likely to fail by analyzing data from sensors and monitoring equipment performance. This allows manufacturers to perform maintenance before a failure occurs, reducing downtime and repair costs.

Quality Control: AI systems are used to monitor production lines in real-time to ensure that products meet quality standards. These systems can detect defects in products, ensuring that only high-quality goods are shipped to customers.

19.9 Ethical Considerations in AI-Driven Business

As businesses increasingly rely on AI, ethical considerations must be taken into account to ensure that AI is used responsibly and fairly.

Data Privacy: AI systems rely on vast amounts of customer data, raising concerns about privacy. Businesses must ensure that they are transparent about how customer data is collected and used, and that appropriate measures are in place to protect sensitive information.

Bias and Fairness: AI algorithms can sometimes reflect the biases present in the data they are trained on. This can lead to discriminatory outcomes, particularly in areas such as recruitment, credit scoring, and lending. It is essential for businesses to ensure that their AI systems are fair, unbiased, and inclusive.

Transparency and Accountability: Businesses must ensure that AI-driven decisions are transparent and accountable. If an AI system makes an error, it is important to understand how and why that decision was made, and who is responsible for it.

19.10 The Future of AI in Business

AI is expected to continue transforming the business landscape, with more organizations adopting AI technologies to improve efficiency, enhance customer experiences, and drive innovation. In the future, AI could play an even greater role in decision-making, automation, and business strategy, leading to smarter, more agile organizations.

AI-Powered Business Models: In the future, AI may help businesses develop entirely new business models by enabling greater automation, improving supply chain management, and providing real-time insights into customer behavior. AI-driven businesses could operate with minimal human intervention, allowing companies to scale rapidly and efficiently.

AI-Driven Innovation: As AI technologies evolve, businesses will have more opportunities to create innovative products and services. By leveraging AI, companies can tap into new markets, create personalized experiences, and stay ahead of the competition.

Chapter 20: AI in Healthcare: Revolutionizing Medicine and Patient Care

Artificial Intelligence (AI) has made significant strides in healthcare, transforming the way we diagnose, treat, and manage diseases. From personalized medicine to robotic surgery, AI is revolutionizing healthcare systems worldwide. In this chapter, we will explore the various ways in which AI is reshaping the healthcare industry, the benefits it offers, and the challenges it presents.

20.1 AI in Disease Diagnosis

One of the most promising applications of AI in healthcare is in disease diagnosis. AI algorithms can analyze medical images, such as X-rays, CT scans, and MRIs, with high accuracy, often detecting conditions that may be missed by human doctors. AI systems can also analyze patient data, such as lab results and medical history, to identify potential health risks and diagnose diseases at an early stage.

Medical Imaging: AI-powered systems use deep learning techniques to analyze medical images and detect abnormalities such as tumors, fractures, or infections. These AI tools can provide a second opinion, improving diagnostic accuracy and helping radiologists identify issues more efficiently.

Early Detection of Diseases: AI systems can analyze patient data to identify early signs of diseases such as cancer, diabetes, or cardiovascular conditions. By detecting these conditions early, AI can help doctors intervene before the disease becomes more severe, improving patient outcomes.

20.2 AI in Personalized Medicine

Personalized medicine is an approach to healthcare that tailors treatments to individual patients based on their genetic makeup, lifestyle, and environmental factors. AI plays a crucial role in this field by analyzing vast amounts of patient data to identify the most effective treatments for each individual.

Genomic Medicine: AI is used to analyze genetic data and identify genetic mutations that may contribute to diseases. By understanding a patient's genetic predispositions, doctors can recommend personalized treatments that are more likely to be effective, reducing the trial-and-error approach to prescribing medications.

Predicting Treatment Responses: AI can predict how patients will respond to specific treatments based on their unique characteristics. This helps doctors make more informed decisions about which medications or therapies are most likely to work for each patient, improving treatment outcomes and reducing side effects.

20.3 AI in Drug Discovery and Development

AI is revolutionizing the process of drug discovery by speeding up the identification of potential drug candidates and optimizing clinical trial designs. AI algorithms can analyze large datasets to identify molecules that have the potential to become effective drugs, reducing the time and cost associated with traditional drug development processes.

Drug Repurposing: AI can identify existing drugs that could be repurposed for new medical conditions. By analyzing data on drug interactions and disease mechanisms, AI can suggest new uses for approved drugs, potentially saving years of research and development time.

Clinical Trials Optimization: AI can help optimize clinical trial designs by identifying the best candidates for trials, predicting patient outcomes, and analyzing data in real-time. This can lead to faster trials, lower costs, and more effective treatments being brought to market.

20.4 AI in Robotics and Surgery

Robotic surgery, powered by AI, is transforming the way surgeries are performed. AI-driven robots assist surgeons in performing complex procedures with precision and accuracy, reducing the risk of human error and improving patient recovery times. These robots can perform minimally invasive procedures, which are less traumatic for patients and result in quicker recovery.

Robot-Assisted Surgery: AI-powered robotic systems, such as the da Vinci Surgical System, enable surgeons to perform surgeries with enhanced precision, flexibility, and control. These systems provide real-time feedback, helping surgeons make better decisions during procedures and reducing the risk of complications.

Minimally Invasive Surgery: AI-driven robots are used in minimally invasive procedures, where small incisions are made instead of large openings. These procedures are less painful, require less recovery time, and carry a lower risk of infection compared to traditional surgeries.

20.5 AI in Virtual Health Assistants

Virtual health assistants powered by AI are becoming increasingly popular in patient care. These assistants can provide health advice, monitor patient symptoms, and even help patients manage chronic conditions from the comfort of their own homes. AI-based virtual assistants are also used to remind patients to take their medications and attend follow-up appointments.

Personal Health Monitoring: AI-driven virtual assistants can monitor a patient's health in real-time by tracking vital signs, such as heart rate, blood pressure, and blood glucose levels. This allows doctors to remotely monitor their patients and intervene if necessary, reducing the need for frequent in-person visits.

Chronic Disease Management: For patients with chronic conditions, AI virtual assistants can help manage symptoms and provide personalized care recommendations. These assistants can remind patients to take medications, provide lifestyle tips, and track symptoms over time, improving patient engagement and outcomes.

20.6 AI in Healthcare Administration

AI is not only improving patient care but also streamlining healthcare administration. From automating administrative tasks to optimizing hospital operations, AI is making healthcare systems more efficient and cost-effective.

Medical Record Management: AI is used to manage electronic health records (EHRs), reducing the time healthcare providers spend on administrative tasks. AI can automate the process of updating patient records, ensuring that all information is accurate and up-to-date.

Optimizing Hospital Operations: AI is used to optimize hospital operations by predicting patient admission rates, managing staff schedules, and ensuring that resources, such as medical equipment and hospital beds, are allocated efficiently. This helps reduce waiting times, improve patient satisfaction, and reduce operational costs.

20.7 AI in Telemedicine

Telemedicine is an increasingly popular form of healthcare delivery, especially in remote areas where access to healthcare facilities may be limited. AI is enhancing telemedicine by enabling remote diagnosis, personalized treatment, and continuous monitoring of patients' health.

Remote Diagnosis: AI-powered systems are capable of analyzing patient data during telemedicine consultations to assist healthcare providers in diagnosing conditions remotely. These systems can suggest possible diagnoses, flag potential issues, and recommend next steps for treatment.

Continuous Monitoring: AI systems can monitor patients in real-time during telemedicine sessions, providing continuous data on vital signs and other health metrics. This allows doctors to adjust treatment plans as needed and provide proactive care to patients.

20.8 AI in Mental Health

AI is also making an impact in the field of mental health, helping to diagnose and treat mental health conditions, such as depression, anxiety, and PTSD. AI tools can analyze patient conversations, behavior patterns, and even facial expressions to assess mental health status and recommend treatment options.

Mental Health Chatbots: AI-powered chatbots are being used to provide mental health support to individuals who may not have access to traditional therapy. These chatbots can engage in conversations, provide emotional support, and offer coping strategies for individuals dealing with stress, anxiety, or depression.

Behavioral Analysis: AI can analyze patterns in a patient's behavior, such as sleep patterns, speech patterns, or activity levels, to detect signs of mental health issues. By monitoring these patterns, AI can help identify early signs of mental health problems and suggest interventions.

20.9 Ethical Considerations in AI Healthcare Applications

As AI continues to play a larger role in healthcare, ethical concerns must be addressed to ensure that AI is used responsibly and equitably.

Data Privacy: Healthcare data is highly sensitive, and protecting patient privacy is crucial. AI systems must comply with strict data privacy regulations, such as HIPAA (Health Insurance Portability and Accountability Act), to ensure that patient information is kept confidential.

Bias and Fairness: AI algorithms can sometimes be biased, depending on the data they are trained on. This can lead to disparities in healthcare outcomes, particularly for marginalized groups. It is important to ensure that AI systems are trained on diverse and representative datasets to avoid bias.

Accountability: If an AI system makes an incorrect diagnosis or treatment recommendation, it is essential to determine who is responsible for the outcome. Establishing clear accountability frameworks is crucial to ensure that AI-driven healthcare systems are reliable and trustworthy.

The future of AI in healthcare looks promising, with advancements in machine learning, natural language processing, and robotics continuing to reshape the industry. AI is expected to play an even greater role in personalized medicine, predictive analytics, and patient care in the coming years.

AI-Driven Healthcare Models: AI has the potential to create new healthcare delivery models, where treatments are more personalized, accessible, and efficient. This could include AI-driven diagnostics, telemedicine, and virtual health assistants, leading to more affordable and accessible healthcare for everyone.

AI-Powered Health Ecosystem: In the future, AI could integrate various aspects of healthcare, including medical research, patient care, and administrative tasks, into a seamless and efficient system. This interconnected ecosystem could lead to more accurate diagnoses, faster treatment times, and better overall patient outcomes.

Chapter 21: The Dangers and Limitations of AI

Introduction

Artificial Intelligence (AI) is revolutionizing industries, automating tasks, and enhancing human capabilities. However, as AI becomes more powerful, it also presents significant risks and limitations. From ethical concerns to security threats, understanding these dangers is crucial for ensuring responsible AI development. In this chapter, we will explore the major risks and limitations of AI.

1. The Dangers of AI

1.1 Job Loss Due to Automation

One of the biggest concerns about AI is its impact on employment. As AI systems replace human workers in various industries, millions of jobs are at risk. While AI creates new opportunities, the transition may lead to widespread unemployment in the short term.

→ **Example**: Automated assembly lines, self-checkout systems, and AI-driven customer support are reducing the need for human workers.

1.2 Bias and Discrimination

AI systems are trained on data, and if this data contains biases, the AI will replicate and even amplify them. This can lead to discrimination in hiring, lending, law enforcement, and other critical areas.

→ **Example**: AI-driven hiring systems have been found to favor certain demographics while discriminating against others due to biased training data.

1.3 Privacy and Data Security Risks

AI relies on vast amounts of data, often including personal and sensitive information. If not properly secured, this data can be exploited by hackers, corporations, or governments, leading to privacy violations.

→ **Example**: Facial recognition AI used for surveillance can track individuals without their consent, raising ethical and legal concerns.

1.4 AI in Cyber Warfare and Autonomous Weapons

AI is being integrated into military and cybersecurity systems, increasing the risk of AI-powered attacks. Autonomous drones, AI-driven hacking tools, and automated defense systems can escalate conflicts and make warfare more unpredictable.

→ **Example**: AI-powered cyberattacks can target financial systems, power grids, and government databases, leading to large-scale disruptions.

1.5 The Risk of Superintelligent AI

If AI surpasses human intelligence, it could become uncontrollable. A highly advanced AI system might act in ways that humans cannot predict or manage, leading to existential risks.

→ **Example**: Prominent figures like Elon Musk and the late Stephen Hawking have warned about the dangers of AI surpassing human intelligence without proper safeguards.

2. Limitations of AI

2.1 Lack of Creativity and Emotional Intelligence

AI can analyze data and recognize patterns, but it lacks true creativity and emotional understanding. While AI can mimic human emotions, it does not genuinely experience them, which limits its ability to handle complex human interactions.

→ **Example**: AI can generate music or paintings based on patterns, but it cannot create original, emotionally driven art like a human artist.

2.2 Absence of Common Sense and Contextual Understanding

AI lacks human-like common sense and struggles with ambiguous or unpredictable situations. It can process data but often fails to understand real-world complexities.

→ **Example**: A self-driving car might fail to interpret an unusual road situation that is not present in its training data.

2.3 High Energy Consumption and Costs

Training and maintaining advanced AI models require significant computational resources, making AI development expensive and environmentally taxing.

→ **Example**: Training large AI models like GPT-4 requires electricity equivalent to powering a small city.

2.4 Ethical and Legal Challenges

AI systems can make decisions, but who is responsible when those decisions go wrong? The lack of clear regulations around AI accountability raises ethical and legal dilemmas.

⊡→ **Example**: If an AI-driven medical diagnosis system makes a fatal mistake, should the blame fall on the developer, the healthcare provider, or the AI itself?

Conclusion

While AI offers groundbreaking advancements, its dangers and limitations must be carefully managed. Ethical AI development, transparency, and regulatory oversight are essential to ensuring that AI benefits society while minimizing risks. As AI continues to evolve, addressing these concerns will be crucial for a safer and more balanced future.

-DR. VIJAY YADAV

www.ingramcontent.com/pod-product-compliance
Lightning Source LLC
LaVergne TN
LVHW051701050326
832903LV00032B/3937